Gulliver's Travels

CBSE Class IX

English-Hindi

ARIHANT PRAKASHAN, MEERUT

ARIHANT PRAKASHAN, MEERUT

卐 Administrative & Production Offices

Corporate Office 4577/15, Agarwal Road, Darya Ganj, New Delhi -110002
Tele: 011- 47630600, 23280316; Fax: 011- 23280316

Head Office Kalindi, TP Nagar, Meerut (UP) - 250002
Tele: 0121-2401479; Fax: 0121-2401648

卐 Sales & Support Offices

Agra, Ahmedabad, Bengaluru, Bhubaneswar, Chennai, Delhi(I&II), Guwahati, Haldwani, Hyderabad, Jaipur, Kolkata, Kota, Lucknow, Nagpur, Meerut, Patna & Pune

卐 ISBN 978-93-5176-967-5

Typeset by Arihant DTP Unit at Meerut
Printed and bound in India at Repro Knowledgecast Limited, Thane

For further information about the products from Arihant,
log on to www.arihantbooks.com or email to info@arihantbooks.com

Preface

The CBSE, in order to develop the habit of long-text reading in students, has introduced this novel in curriculum of class IX English Communicative and English Language and Literature. This book is prescribed keeping in view the lightness of the text and simplicity of the plot of the novel so that students will enjoy reading it.

Gullivers Travels (1726, amended 1735), is a novel by Irish writer and clergyman Jonathan Swift, that is both a satire on human nature and a parody of the travellers tales literary

sub-genre. It is Swifts best known full-length work, and a classic of English literature. The book became popular as soon as it was published. John Gay wrote in a 1726 letter to Swift that It is universally read, from the cabinet council to the nursery. Since then, it has never been out of print.

Cavehill in Belfast is thought to be the inspiration for the novel. Swift imagined that the mountain resembled the shape of a sleeping giant safeguarding the city. Jonathan Swift became a national hero for defending Ireland against the inequities of the English whigs.

This series has been specially prepared with the purpose to make the reading of novels easy and less time consuming. The novel has been covered in English & Hindi Language both because reading in English is takes more time than in Hindi. For this reason, we have tried to make the reading easy by giving the material in both Hindi & English Language, so that the students can understand the content of the novels in a comfortable way and then write the perfect answers.

We have tried to help out the students in all aspects to learn this novel in such a way so that they will become competent enough to answer the questions that will come in exams. We hope the student will relish this book.

Novel Outline

- About the Novel vi-vii
- Know the Characters viii-xi

Term - I

Part I A Voyage to Lilliput

Chapter 1 2-5

Chapter 2 6-9

Chapter 3 10-13

Chapter 4 14-17

Chapter 5 18-23

Chapter 6 24-25

Chapter 7 26-27

Chapter 8 28-29

Part II A Voyage to Brobdingnag

Chapter 1 30-31

Chapter 2 32-35

Chapter 3 36-39

Chapter 4 40-43

Chapter 5 44-45

Chapter 6 46-49

Chapter 7 50-53

Chapter 8 54-57

- **Question Digest** **58-61**

Term - II

Part III A Voyage to Laputa, Balnibarbi Luggnag, Glubbdubdrib and Japan

Chapter 1	62-67
Chapter 2	68-71
Chapter 3	72-73
Chapter 4	74-77
Chapter 5	78-83
Chapter 6	84-85
Chapter 7	86-87
Chapter 8	88-91
Chapter 9	92-95
Chapter 10	96-99
Chapter 11	100-101

Part IV A Voyage to the Country of the Houyhnhnm

Chapter 1	102-105
Chapter 2	106-109
Chapter 3	110-111
Chapter 4	112-113
Chapter 5	114-117
Chapter 6	118-121
Chapter 7	122-125
Chapter 8	126-129
Chapter 9	130-135
Chapter 10	136-139
Chapter 11	140-145
Chapter 12	146-149

- **Question Digest** **150-155**
- **Character Sketches** **156-160**

About the Novel

Gulliver, a ship surgeon, was lost in the sea due to a mishap in the voyage and he found himself on a very lonely island where he met people and animal of unusual sizes. He spent days over there and returned safely to England, his native place.

When Gulliver was on the voyage his ship was wrecked due to a heavy storm and he ended up in landing an island of Lilliput. The inhabitants of Lilliput, called Lillipution were strange people and their height was merely six inches. Gulliver was lying in an unconscious state and was surrounded by those Lilliputians. The smaller people greeted him and showed their concern to Gulliver. In the reciprocation, Gulliver helped them. He ended the ever-long conflict between Lilliput and the other island Blefuscu. He refused to fulfil the desire of the king of Lilliput to enslave the Blefuscu and he left the island for good. He went to Blefuscu and used a warship for his own use to sail from there and to reach England anyways.

After reaching England safely he was again sent on an island with a small crew to find the possibility of water there. As they all reached the island they came to know that it was the island of giants. Seeing the giants all the crew members flee from there, but Gulliver was captured by a farmer. The farmer brought him to his home and took all the great care. He left him in the custody of his daughter and when he came back he took him out and displayed him before the passers-by. Finally Gulliver was sold to the queen. Gulliver met the king in the court and both discussed various issues related to custom and culture what the king thought mean. Gulliver was kept under a box and one day he was looking at the sea, an eagle snatched him up and dropped in the sea where he was rescued by a ship and he again reached England.

Next time, Gulliver found himself on a ship that was scheduled for Levant. When they reach there, Gulliver was made captain of the sloop so that they can visit nearby islands and they could establish trade there. The sloop was attacked by the pirates and Gulliver was placed in a boat that was drifting in the sea. Drifting in the sea for a long time Gulliver reached a flying island Laputa from where he visited many islands and finally reached Japan from where he reached to England again.

Next time Gulliver was made the captain of a merchant ship that was heading towards Barbados. Many of the crew members fell ill during the voyage and ultimately died. That forced Gulliver to hire some other sailors so that the voyage might continue. But one of the hired sailors was a pirate and he provoked the others to rebel and they all ransacked the ship from Gulliver and took away all the consignment Gulliver was left behind and later on attacked by a herd of ugly looking creature called Yahoos. Finally, Gulliver again managed to return to England.

Novel के बारे में...

गुलिवर, जो एक जहाज पर सर्जन था, एक समुद्री यात्रा के दौरान आए तूफान की वजह से समुद्र में खो जाता है। बाद में किसी द्वीप पर वह अजीबोगरीब किस्म के प्राणियों से मिलता है। कुछ दिन वहाँ पर व्यतीत करने के पश्चात् वह वापस इंग्लैंड आ जाता है।

जब गुलिवर समुद्री यात्रा पर जाता है तो उसका जहाज तूफान का शिकार हो जाता है और वह लिलिपुटियन के द्वारा पकड़ लिया जाता है। लिलिपुटियन छोटी ऊँचाई वाले लोग थे तथा उन लोगों ने गुलिवर का बहुत ध्यान रखा। बदले में गुलिवर ने उनकी मदद की और एक दूसरे द्वीप के लोगों से उनके लंबे समय से चले आ रहे हैं विवाद को समाप्त करवा दिया। बाद में वह एक युद्धपोत, जो टूट चुका था, की मदद से वापस इंग्लैंड चला आता है।

अगली बार जब गुलिवर समुद्री यात्रा पर जाता है तो वह अपने दल के साथ पानी की तलाश में निकलता है। इस बार उसका सामना विशालकाय जीवों से होता है जिन्हें देखकर उस के दल के अन्य सदस्य भाग जाते हैं और गुलिवर को पकड़ लिया जाता है। उसे लोगों के सामने प्रस्तुत किया जाता है तथा अंततः उसे रानी को बेच दिया जाता है। राजा के साथ गुलिवर की लंबी चर्चा के दौरान वह रीति-रिवाजों तथा संस्कारों की चर्चा करता है। गुलिवर को एक बक्से में बंद करके रखा जाता है और एक गिद्ध द्वारा उसे झपट्टा मारकर समुद्र में गिरा दिया जाता है। वहाँ से गुलिवर एक समुद्री जहाज के द्वारा बचा लिया जाता है तथा सुरक्षित इंग्लैंड आ जाता है।

एक अन्य समुद्री यात्रा के दौरान गुलिवर लेवांट की ओर जाने वाला होता है। वहाँ पहुँचने के बाद गुलिवर को वहाँ का कैप्टन बना दिया जाता है ताकि वे लोग वहाँ पर किसी व्यापार की संभावना तलाश करें। वहाँ पर समुद्री डाकुओं का हमला होता है और गुलिवर को एक नाव में बाँधकर समुद्र में भटकने हेतु छोड़ दिया जाता है। भटकते हुए गुलिवर जापान और फिर वहाँ से इंग्लैड आ जाता है।

आखिरी समुद्री यात्रा में गुलिवर को समुद्री व्यापारिक जहाज का कप्तान बना दिया जाता है जो बारबाडोस की तरफ जा रहा था। गुलिवर के दल के कई सदस्य समुद्री बीमारी की वजह से मारे गए। मजबूरीवश गुलिवर को अन्य नाविकों से मदद लेनी पड़ी। नाविकों में से एक, जो डाकू था, अन्य नाविकों को विद्रोह के लिए उकसाया तथा उन लोगों ने जहाज को लूट लिया। बाद में गुलिवर पर याहू का हमला होता है जो बदसूरत से दिखने वाले प्राणी थे। अंततः गुलिवर वापस इंग्लैंड आ जाता है।

Know the **Characters...**

Gullivers

The narrator and protagonist of the story. Although Lemuel Gulliver's vivid and detailed style of narration makes it clear that he is intelligent and well - educated, his perceptions are naïve and gullible. He has virtually no emotional life, or at least no awareness of it and his comments are strictly factual. Indeed, sometimes his obsession with the facts of navigation, for example, becomes unbearable for us, as his fictional editor, Richard Sympson, makes clear when he explains having had to cut out nearly half of Gullivers verbiage. Gulliver never thinks that the absurdities he encounters are funny and never makes the satiric connections between the lands he visits and his own home. Gullivers naïveté makes the satire possible, as we pick up on things that Gulliver does not notice.

The Emperor

The ruler of Lilliput. Like all Lilliputians, the emperor is fewer than six inches tall. His power and majesty impress Gulliver deeply, but to us he appears both laughable and sinister. Because of his tiny size, his belief that he can control Gulliver seems silly, but his willingness to execute his subjects for minor reasons of politics or honour gives him a frightening aspect. He is proud of possessing the tallest trees and biggest palace in the kingdom, but he is also quite hospitable, spending a fortune on his captives food. The emperor is both a satire of the autocratic ruler and a strangely serious portrait of political power.

The Farmer

Gullivers first master in Brobdingnag. The farmer speaks to Gulliver, showing that he is willing to believe that the relatively tiny Gulliver may be as rational as he himself is, and treats him with gentleness. However, the farmer puts Gulliver on display around Brobdingnag, which clearly shows that he would rather profit from his discovery than converse with him as an equal. His exploitation of Gulliver as a labourer, which nearly starves Gulliver to death, seems less cruel than simple minded. Generally, the farmer represents the average Brobdingnagian of no great gifts or intelligence, wielding an extraordinary power over Gulliver simply by virtue of his immense size.

Glumdalclitch

The farmers nine years old daughter, who is forty feet tall. Glumdalclitch becomes Gullivers friend and nurse-maid, hanging him to sleep safely in her closet at night and teaching him the Brobdingnagian language by day. She is skilled at sewing and makes Gulliver several sets of new clothes, taking delight in dressing him. When the queen discovers that no one at court is suited to care for Gulliver, she invites Glumdalclitch to live at court as his sole babysitter, a function she performs with great seriousness and attentiveness. To Glumdalclitch, Gulliver is basically a living doll, symbolising the general status Gulliver has in Brobdingnag.

The Queen

The queen of Brobdingnag, who is so delighted by Gulliver's beauty and charms that she agrees to buy him from the farmer for 1000 pieces of gold. Gulliver appreciates her kindness after the hardships he suffers at the farmer's and shows his usual fawning love for royalty by kissing the tip of her little finger when presented before her. She possesses, in Gullivers words, "infinite" wit and humour, though this description may entail a bit of Gullivers characteristic flattery of superiors. The queen seems genuinely considerate, asking Gulliver whether he would consent to live at court instead of simply taking him in as a pet and inquiring into the reasons for his cold good-byes with the farmer. She is by no means a hero, but simply a pleasant, powerful person.

Novel में उपस्थित प्रमुख व्यक्ति

गुलिवर

कथावाचक एवं कहानी का मुख्य नायक। यद्यपि लैमुअल गुलिवर के कथा कहने के तरीके से पता चलता है कि वह भली-भाँति शिक्षित एवं दूरदर्शी सोच वाला व्यक्ति है किंतु कहीं-कहीं उसके विचार उसके अनुभवहीन एवं सरल व्यक्तित्व वाला होने की पुष्टि करते हैं। आभासी रूप से उसकी कोई भावनात्मक जिंदगी नहीं अथवा उसे भावनाओं का कोई ज्ञान नहीं है एवं उसके विचार पूर्ण रूप से तार्किक हैं। वास्तव में कहीं-कहीं नौका विज्ञान से उसके लगाव से संबंधित तथ्य हमें बोझिल लगने लगते हैं परंतु उसके संपादक रिचर्ड सिंपसन का प्रस्तुतीकरण विषय को सहज बनाता है जिसमें उस संपादक ने गुलिवर के अनावश्यक विचारों को पृथक् कर दिया है। गुलिवर कभी यह नहीं सोचता कि वह जिन विषमताओं का सामना कर रहा है, वे हास्यास्पद हैं तथा वह कभी भी उन परिस्थितियों की अपने गृहनगर से व्यंग्यपूर्ण तुलना भी नहीं करता है। यद्यपि गुलिवर की सरलता व्यंग्य का अवसर उत्पन्न करती है, विशेष रूप से उन बातों के संदर्भ में जिन पर गुलिवर का ध्यान नहीं जाता।

बादशाह

लिलिपुट का बादशाह एवं अन्य लिलिपुट वासियों की भाँति बादशाह भी छः इंच से कम लंबाई वाला है। उसकी ताकत एवं सत्ता गुलिवर को प्रभावित करती है परंतु हमारे लिए वह हँसी तथा डरावना पात्र है। उसके छोटे कद के बावजूद उसका विश्वास कि वह गुलिवर को नियंत्रित कर लेगा, मूर्खतापूर्ण लगता है परंतु राजनीति या सम्मान से जुड़े छोटे मुद्दों पर भी अपराधियों का मृत्युदंड देने की उसकी प्रवृत्ति उसे डरावना बनाती है। उसे अपने साम्राज्य में सबसे बड़े होने पर गर्व है तथा उसका राज्य बड़ा है, इस बात का भी उसे गर्व है परंतु वह अपने बंदी बनाए हुए व्यक्तियों के भोजन पर उदारतापूर्वक व्यय करता है जो उसकी उदार मनोवृत्ति का परिचायक है। बादशाह एक तानाशाही शासक तथा राजनैतिक शक्ति का प्रतीक दोनों ही है।

कृषक

ब्रॉबडिंगनाग में गुलिवर का प्रथम स्वामी। कृषक गुलिवर से बातें करता है तथा यह प्रदर्शित करता है कि वह यह स्वीकार करने को राजी है कि कद में अत्यंत छोटा गुलिवर भी उसकी तरह ही आनुपातिक व्यवहार वाला हो सकता है तथा कृषक उसके प्रति यथोचित व्यवहार करता है। यद्यपि बाद में कृषक गुलिवर को प्रदर्शनी हेतु रखता है जिससे यह स्पष्ट हो जाता है कि वह गुलिवर से समतापूर्ण व्यवहार करने के स्थान पर उससे लाभ कमाना अधिक पसंद करेगा। उसका गुलिवर के प्रति शोषणकारी व्यवहार जो कि लगभग गुलिवर को मृत्यु तक ले जाता है, हमें सामान्य रूप से सोचने पर अधिक क्रूरतापूर्ण नहीं प्रतीत होता है। सामान्य रूप से कहा जाए तो गुलिवर का स्वामी कृषक एक सामान्य ब्रॉबडिंगनाग वासी है जिसके पास कोई अतिरिक्त विशेषता नहीं है तथा उसे अपने असाधारण आकार के कारण ही गुलिवर से अधिक शक्ति प्राप्त है।

ग्लमडैलक्लिच

कृषक की नौ वर्षीय पुत्री जिसका कद 40 फीट है। ग्लमडैलक्लिच गुलिवर की मित्र एवं सहायक परिचारिका बन जाती है तथा वह उसे उसकी सुरक्षा हेतु रात में अपने पलंग में सुलाती है तथा दिन में उसे ब्रॉबडिंगनाग की भाषा सिखाती है। उसे सिलाई कला में दक्षता प्राप्त है तथा वह गुलिवर के लिए कई नए कपड़े सिलती है तथा इस कार्य में उसे आनंद प्राप्त होता है। जब रानी को यह ज्ञात हो जाता है कि दरबार में कोई भी गुलिवर का ध्यान ठीक तरह से रख सकने में सक्षम नहीं है तो वह ग्लमडैलक्लिच को दरबार में आने का निमंत्रण देती है तथा उसे गुलिवर की देख-रेख की जिम्मेदारी सौंपती है जिसे ग्लमडैलक्लिच पूरी तन्मयता तथा गंभीरता के साथ निभाती है। ग्लमडैलक्लिच हेतु गुलिवर एक जीती-जागती गुड़िया है तथा ब्रॉबडिंगनाग में गुलिवर की सामान्य पहचान भी यही है।

रानी

ब्रॉबडिंगनाग की रानी गुलिवर की सुंदरता एवं उसके आकर्षण से अत्यधिक सम्मोहित हो जाती है तथा वह उसे 1,000 स्वर्ण मुद्राओं के बदले कृषक से खरीद लेती है। गुलिवर रानी की दयालुता की प्रशंसा करता है तथा कृषक के द्वारा किए गए क्रूर व्यवहार के पश्चात् जब उसे रानी का स्नेहपूर्ण व्यवहार मिलता है तो वह भावविहवल हो जाता है। जब उसे रानी के समक्ष प्रस्तुत किया जाता है तब वह रानी की छोटी उंगली का चुंबन लेकर रानी के प्रति अपने प्रेम व आदर को प्रकट करता है। गुलिवर के शब्दों में रानी के पास ''असाधारण वृद्धि एवं विनोदप्रियता'' थी, यद्यपि यह विवरण हमें गुलिवर के विशिष्ट व्यक्तियों की चापलूसी करने के स्वभाव की थोड़ी सी झलक भी देता है। रानी पर्याप्त रूप से विचारशील है क्योंकि वह गुलिवर से पूछती है कि क्या वह दरबार में रहना पसंद करेगा बजाय इसके कि वह पालतू बनकर रानी के साथ रहे तथा वह उससे उसके कृषक के प्रति रूखे व्यवहार के विषय में भी पूछती है। वह किसी भी प्रकार से नायिका नहीं है परंतु वह एक आनंददायक तथा शक्तिशाली व्यक्तित्व की स्वामिनी है।

Gulliver's Travels

Part I 1

Early Days

Gulliver has been a student of Cambridge. Gulliver joins Mr James Bates, a London surgeon, as a learner. Later, he travels to Leyden, having a university famous for its teaching of medicine.

First Voyage on the Ship—The Swallow and Marriage

After studying here for some years, he comes back to England. Having travelled for three years on the Swallow, Gulliver returns to London and marries Mary Burton who arrives with a handsome dowry of 400 pounds. In the long run, Mr Bates dies and unfortunately, Gulliver's business deteriorates day-by-day.

On the Antelope Ship—Second and Decisive Voyage

He joins the ship the Antelope, with Captain William Prichard, but here too ship gets wrecked. Twelve members die while the rest were weakened by the excessive labour and starvation.

Captivated by the Lilliputians

Gulliver swims to the shore. When he wakes up from sleep, he finds himself tied with pieces of thread. He feels something moving over his body. He is surprised to see little people climb his body. He is in the land of Lilliput.

Word Meaning

Scanty	– अल्प	Eminent	– प्रसिद्ध
Voyage	– समुद्री यात्रा	Fortunate	– सौभाग्यशाली
Immoderate	– अत्यधिक	Computation	– गणना
Ligature	– पट्टी	Striving	– प्रयासरत

1

प्रारंभिक दिन

Gulliver (गुलिवर) Cambridge University (कैम्ब्रिज विश्वविद्यालय) का छात्र रहा। गुलिवर ने Mr James Bates (श्रीमान जेम्स बेट्स) जोकि London (लंदन) के एक शल्य चिकित्सक थे, का प्रशिक्षु बनने का निर्णय लिया। कुछ समय पश्चात् उसने Leyden (लेडेन) की यात्रा की, जो अपने चिकित्सा विश्वविद्यालय हेतु प्रसिद्ध था।

स्वालो जहाज-प्रथम समुद्री यात्रा एवं विवाह

कुछ समय तक अध्ययन के पश्चात् वह वापस England (इंग्लैंड) लौट गया। Swallow (स्वालो) जहाज पर तीन वर्षों तक कार्य करने के पश्चात् गुलिवर वापस लंदन आ गया एवं उसने Mary Burton (मैरी बर्टन) से विवाह कर लिया जो उसके लिए दहेज के रूप में 400 पाउंड लेकर आई थी। कालांतर में Mr Bates (श्रीमान बेट्स) का देहावसान हो गया एवं दुर्भाग्यवश गुलिवर का व्यापार दिन-प्रतिदिन बिगड़ने लगा।

एंटीलोप जहाज-द्वितीय एवं निर्णायक समुद्री यात्रा

उसने Antelope (एंटीलोप) नामक जहाज पर कप्तान William Prichard (विलियम प्रिचर्ड) के साथ यात्रा प्रारंभ की, परंतु उसका जहाज ध्वस्त हो गया। जहाज के सदस्यों में से बारह की मृत्यु हो गई तथा अन्य सदस्य थकान एवं Starvation (भुखमरी) के कारण कमजोर होते गए।

लिलिपुटवासियों द्वारा बंदी बना लिया जाना

गुलिवर किनारे पर तैरकर पहुँच जाता है। जब वह नींद से जागता है तो वह स्वयं को धागे के टुकड़ों द्वारा बँधा हुआ पाता है। वह अपने शरीर पर किसी वस्तु के चलने को महसूस करता है। वह छोटे-छोटे मनुष्यों को अपने शरीर पर चढ़ते हुए देखकर आश्चर्यचकित हो जाता है। वह लिलिपुट की जमीन पर है।

Permit	– अनुमति	Famished	– भूखा
Dexterity	– कुशलता	Intrepidity	– निडरता
Prodigious	– आश्चर्यजनक	Dart	– भाला

Important Questions

Questions based on the Plot of the Chapter

Q 1. Describe Gulliver's life before he undertook a voyage on the ship, the Antelope.

एंटीलोप जहाज पर समुद्री यात्रा से पूर्व गुलिवर के जीवन का वर्णन करिए।

गुलिवर का कैम्ब्रिज का विद्यार्थी होना – स्वयं के लिए संभावनाएँ तलाशना – दुर्भाग्यवश, पिता की आर्थिक स्थिति खराब होना – उसे कैम्ब्रिज छोड़ने हेतु विवश होना – कुछ समय पश्चात् प्रशिक्षु के तौर पर उसका श्रीमान बेट्स के पास जाना – उसका गणित एवं नौसंचालन विषयों को पढ़ना – लेडेन जाकर चिकित्सा का अध्ययन करना एवं वापस आकर 'स्वालो' जहाज पर चिकित्सक के रूप में कार्य करना – बाद में मैरी बर्टन से विवाह करना – श्रीमान बेट्स की मृत्यु एवं व्यापार में घाटा होना।

Ans. Gulliver was a student of Cambridge and he was trying to find out the scope and career related aspects for himself. Gulliver was the student of a famous institute, so it was not much complex for him to find out a better way for himself. However, everything could not be continued in a usual way and because of the deteriorating financial condition of his father, Gulliver had to discontinue his studies. This was a turning point for him because he had to join Mr James Bates, a London surgeon, as a learner in order to continue his learning and normal living. Gulliver studied mathematics and navigation. Later he went to Leyden for education of medicine and after returning from Leyden, he joined the crew of a ship named Swallow.

Q 2. Why Gulliver had to go on a voyage again after marriage?

विवाह के पश्चात् किन परिस्थितियों में गुलिवर को समुद्री यात्रा पर जाना पड़ा?

गुलिवर के जीवन का प्रारंभिक दौर उतार-चढ़ाव से भरा होना – उसके द्वारा कैम्ब्रिज में पढ़ाई न जारी रख पाना – आर्थिक मुश्किलों का सामने आना – गुलिवर का इधर-उधर भटकते हुए असतत प्रकार से पढ़ाई जारी रखना – चिकित्सा संबंधी जानकारी प्राप्त करने हेतु उसका लेडेन जाना तथा वहाँ अध्ययन करना – कुछ समय बाद उसका वापस इंग्लैंड आना तथा 'स्वालो' जहाज पर चिकित्सक के रूप में कार्य करना – तीन वर्षों तक कार्य करना एवं उसके पश्चात् लंदन वापस आना – वहाँ उसका विवाह होना – श्रीमान बेट्स का मृत्यु को प्राप्त होना तथा गुलिवर को व्यापार में घाटा होना – उसका पुनः समुद्री यात्रा पर जाना।

Ans. The initial phase of Gulliver's life was quite unstable and filled with various ups and downs. He could not continue his studies in Cambridge because of the worse economic condition of his father. After this, he had to continue his studies in discrete manner by wandering here and there. In order to gain knowledge of medical field, he visited Leyden and there he joined a famous medical university. After sometime, he returned to England and joined the crew of ship the 'Swallow' as a surgeon. He continued his service there for three years and after that, he returned to London where he married del Mary Burton. However, the situation changed after sometime and condition became critical for Gulliver. Mr Bates died and Gulliver's business began to deteriorate slowly. It was a misfortune for him and later he decided to go on a voyage again after almost three years of his marriage.

Question based on the Character Sketch

Q 3. Give a brief character sketch of Gulliver on the basis of the incidents of this chapter.

अध्याय में हुई घटनाओं के आधार पर गुलिवर का संक्षिप्त चरित्र चित्रण करिए।

गुलिवर का दृढ़निश्चित प्रवृत्ति का होना – उसे समुद्री यात्रा में रुचि होना – गुलिवर का निडर व्यक्ति होना – गुलिवर का अनेक बाधाओं का सामना करना – उसका अध्ययन सतत रूप से न हो पाना – स्वयं के प्रयासों से उसका अध्ययन को जारी रखना – गुलिवर का उत्साही व्यक्ति होना – समुद्री यात्रा के प्रति उसका अत्यंत झुकाव होना – उसके द्वारा नौसंचालन विषय का अध्ययन किया जाना – उसके द्वारा कई समुद्री यात्राएँ करना।

Ans. Gulliver was very fond of voyages. He wanted to discover new aspects of the sea and this was his passion. He was a rigid and fearless person.

On the basis of this chapter, we see following traits in his character

A Fearless Person Gulliver had to face various problems during his studies as his family was not economically very strong. However, Gulliver never cared for this and he continued his studies through self efforts.

An Adventurous Person Gulliver was an adventurous person and he wanted to explore the world of sea. So, he studied navigation also in order to get knowledge of voyages and ships. He went on various voyages because of his interest. Thus, we can say that Gulliver was a fearless and adventurous person.

Gulliver at the Ancient Temple

Gulliver is finally allowed to stand up and view the countryside. He finds it beautiful with the tallest trees seven feet in height.

Gulliver Relieves Himself

He is enjoying the beauty of the land, he feels the need to urinate. It has been two days since he last relieved himself. He walks inside the building to the edge of his chain and relieves himself in open air.

Gulliver's Meeting with the Emperor of Lilliput

The emperor one day visits Gulliver on horseback from his tower. He orders his servants to give Gulliver food and drink. Both talk to each other, but do not understand anything. Gulliver is now under the guard of the Lilliputian soldiers. Some of them shoot arrows at him. The Brigadier ties up six of them and places them in Gulliver's hand.

Lilliputians' Hostility

After two weeks, a bed is made for Gulliver. It is made of 600 small beds sewn together. By this time the news of Gulliver's arrival spreads through the kingdom. People from villages come to see him.

He hires 300 tailors to make him clothing. He also offers 6 teachers to instruct Gulliver in their language. After three weeks only, Gulliver is well conversant with their language and is able to converse with the emperor. Gulliver also yearns to be free, but he is asked to wear a peace with him and his kingdom.

2

गुलिवर को प्राचीन मंदिर में रखा गया

Gulliver (गुलिवर) को अंत में खड़े होकर Countryside (गाँव) को देखने दिया जाता है। वह सात फुट ऊँचे वृक्षों के साथ इसे सुंदर पाता है।

गुलिवर का स्वयं को संयत करना

गुलिवर प्राकृतिक दृश्यों का आनंद ले रहा था, परंतु उसे Urinate (मूत्र विसर्जन) कर स्वयं को संयत करने की आवश्यकता अनुभव हुई। गुलिवर ने बीते दो दिनों से मूत्र विसर्जन नहीं किया था। गुलिवर अपनी जंजीर में रहते हुए भवन के अंदर गया तथा उसने मुक्त वातावरण में ही मूत्र विसर्जन किया।

गुलिवर की लिलिपुट के सम्राट से मुलाकात

एक दिन अपनी Tower (टावर) से Emperor (सम्राट) घोड़े पर बैठकर गुलिवर के पास जाता है। वह अपने नौकरों को गुलिवर को खाना और शराब देने का आदेश देता है। दोनों आपस में बात करते हैं, परंतु कुछ समझ नहीं आता है। गुलिवर अब लिलिपुट के सैनिकों की देखरेख में है। कुछ उस पर तीर चलाते हैं। Brigadier (ब्रिगेडियर) उनमें से छः को बाँध देता है और गुलिवर के हाथ में रख देता है।

लिलिपुटवासियों का असहनीय व्यवहार

दो सप्ताह पश्चात् गुलिवर के लिए एक Bed (पलंग) बनाया जाता है। वह 600 छोटे पलंगों की एक साथ Sewn (सिलाई) करके बनाया जाता है। इस समय तक गुलिवर के आने का समाचार पूरे सम्राट नगर में फैल जाता है। गाँवों से व्यक्ति उसे देखने के लिए आते हैं।

उसने 300 दर्जियों को गुलिवर हेतु वस्त्र तैयार करने का कार्य दिया। इसके अतिरिक्त गुलिवर को भाषा ज्ञान उपलब्ध कराने हेतु सम्राट ने 6 भाषा विशेषज्ञ अध्यापकों का प्रबंध किया। तीन सप्ताहों की अवधि के पश्चात् ही गुलिवर उनकी भाषा में निपुण हो गया एवं सम्राट से बात करने में सक्षम हो गया। गुलिवर ने मुक्त होकर वापस जाने की इच्छा व्यक्त की, परंतु सम्राट ने उसे शांतिपूर्वक अपने Kingdom (साम्राज्यवासियों) के साथ ही रहने को कहा।

Word Meaning

Prospect	– दृश्य	Necessities	– आवश्यकताएँ
Expedient	– उचित	Candid	– स्पष्ट
Offensive	– अप्रिय	Momentous	– महत्त्वपूर्ण
Maligners	– आलोचक	Alighted	– किसी वाहन से उतरना
Deportment	– व्यवहार	Felicity	– सुख-शांति
Plume	– पंख	Hilt	– तलवार का हत्था
Scabbard	– म्यान	Articulate	– स्पष्ट करना
Smattering	– अल्पज्ञान	Malice	– घृणा
Rabble	– गिरोह	Pikes	– नुकीला हथियार
Squalled	– चीखा	Coverlets	– पलंगपोश
Inured	– अभ्यस्त	Carcase	– पशु का मृत शरीर
Stench	– दुर्गंध, बदबू	Demesnes	– बड़े कमरे से जुड़ी भूमि
Discreet	– समझदार	Inventory	– सूचना संग्रहण
Fobs	– जेब से जुड़ी छोटी जंजीर	Imprimis	– पहले स्थान पर
Substances	– सामग्री	Palisadoes	– दीवार
Lucid	– सुस्पष्ट	Incessant	– निरंतर
Oracle	– देवदूत	Scimitar	– शमशीर
Daunted	– निउत्साहित किया	Kindle	– मोमबत्ती जलाना
Dray-men	– गाड़ी खींचने वाले लोग	Ale	– एक प्रकार की बिअर
Snuff box	– तंबाकू सूँघने की डिब्बी	Perspective	– दृष्टिकोण
Ventured	– जोखिम उठाना		

Important Questions

Questions based on the Plot of the Chapter

Q 1. How did Gulliver relieve himself from nature's call? How did he justify his unclean act?

गुलिवर ने स्वयं को कैसे प्राकृतिक क्रिया से निवृत्त किया? उसने अपने इस गंदगीपूर्ण कार्य को कैसे न्यायोचित ठहराया?

गुलिवर का लिलिपुट द्वीप को अत्यधिक सुंदर पाना – उसे प्राकृतिक क्रिया से निवृत्त होने की आवश्यकता महसूस होना – पैरों में चेन बँधी होना – गुलिवर का प्राचीन मंदिर के भीतर ही इस क्रिया से निवृत्त हो जाना – इस गंदगीपूर्ण कृत्य के लिए स्वयं को अपराधी मानना – अगले समय में उसका खुले स्थान पर प्राकृतिक क्रिया से निवृत्त होना – उसका स्वयं को अत्यधिक असहाय मानना – बंदी होने के कारण स्वतंत्र होकर न घूम पाना।

Ans. The first impression that Gulliver got of Lilliput on looking around was that of beds of flowers. It looked like a painted scene of a city in a theatre. Gulliver now felt the urgent need to urinate. It had been almost two days since he had last disburdened himself. He was under a great difficulty between urgency and shame. Lodged in a deserted ancient temple, he took the first opportunity to relieve himself by answering the call of nature. So, he went into his house as far as the length of his chain would allow and relieved himself.

But he was feeling very guilty of his unclean action. From then on he started relieving himself in open space at the full length of his chain. But he was very helpless at that time and could not do much to avoid it, as he was a captive and could not move freely.

Questions based on the Character Sketch

Q 2. Give the character sketch of the emperor on the basis of your reading of the current chapter.

प्रस्तुत अध्याय के आधार पर लिलिपुट के सम्राट का चरित्र चित्रण कीजिए।

लिलिपुट के सम्राट का तीखे नैन-नक्श वाला, लंबा और अच्छे व्यक्तित्व का व्यक्ति होना – सम्राट का एक गौरवशाली एवं सम्मानित व्यक्ति होना – सम्राट का मुख्यत: अच्छे स्वभाव तथा उदार चरित्र वाला व्यक्ति होना – गुलिवर के लिए रहने तथा खाने का व्यापक प्रबंध करना – गुलिवर से खतरा न होने पर उसे स्वतंत्र कर देना – लोगों को गुलिवर के रास्ते में न आने के लिए कहना – सम्राट का सदा अपनी मंत्रिपरिषद् की सलाह लेना – सलाह के उपयोगी न होने पर उसे खारिज कर देना – मेहमानों व अजनबियों का अतिथि सत्कार करना।

Ans. The emperor of Lilliput was a sharp featured tall man and had a well shaped personality. His countenance is erect and his body and limbs are well-proportioned. He appeared to be very dignified and graceful. The emperor was basically a good natured and generous man. He received Gulliver rather warmly. He made elaborate arrangements for his boarding and lodging. He allowed him to move around the metropolis. After ensuring himself that Gulliver was no threat to him or his kingdom, he granted freedom to him. But he did not allow him to move round the metropolis untill he issued a proclamation. He asked people to be away from Gulliver's route and avoid themselves being crushed by the man-mountain. He was a capable administrator who ran the state with his ministers' advice, but he overruled their suggestions, if he saw no wisdom in them. On the whole, he was a well deserving king who ruled over his people efficiently and treated strangers hospitably.

Diversions

Gulliver hopes to be set free. By this time he has earned the trust of the emperor and his council. Gulliver is entertained with shows like that of Rope-dancers. The dancers dance on ropes. These are slender threads suspended two feet above the ground. It is a kind of competitive examination. Even the Chief Minister and the other ministers have to take part in it to show that they are still fit and skilled.

In another diversion, the emperor lays three silken threads of different colours on a table. He then holds out a stick. Candidates are asked to leap over it or creep under it. Whoever shows the dexterity wins one of the ribbons. Gulliver builds a kind of platform from sticks and handkerchief. He asks the horsemen to exercise on it. The emperor enjoys it.

Gulliver's Hat Discovered Ashore

As Gulliver is busy in diversions, he is informed that a black thing, not looking like a living creature, has washed ashore. He discovers that it was his hat which was left when sailing on the Antelope. It was not in a good condition yet it was looking good. He requests the emperor to command his men to fetch it for him.

Word Meaning

Dexterity	– कुशलता	Diverted	– मनोरंजन
Slender	– पतली	Somersault	– उलट-पलट
Trencher	– लकड़ी का तख्ता	Infallibly	– निश्चित रूप से
Agility	– फुर्ती	Ledges	– ऊँची खड़ी चट्टान
Skirmisher	– सैनिक	Asunder	– टुकड़े-टुकड़े
Patron	– संरक्षक/आश्रयदाता	Entreated	– आग्रह किया
Breeches	– कसी पतलून	Mortal	– जो अमर न हो

3

मनोरंजन

Gulliver (गुलिवर) को स्वतंत्र होने की आशा है। उस समय तक उसने सम्राट को और उसकी परिषद् के विश्वास को अर्जित कर लिया है। गुलिवर का Rope-dancers जैसे Show (शो) के साथ मनोरंजन किया जाता है। नाचने वाले रस्सी पर नाचते हैं। ये जमीन से दो फुट ऊपर लटकाए हुए पतले Thread (धागे) हैं। यह एक प्रकार की प्रतियोगी परीक्षा है। Chief Minister (मुख्यमंत्री) और दूसरे मंत्रियों को ये दिखाने के लिए कि वे अभी भी गुणी और निपुण हैं, इसमें भाग लेना पड़ता है।

अन्य मनोरंजन में सम्राट एक मेज पर अलग-अलग रंग के तीन रेशमी धागों को रखता है। फिर वह एक डंडे को पकड़ता है। प्रतिभागियों को इसके ऊपर कूदने के लिए या इसके नीचे रेंगने के लिए कहा जाता है। जो कोई निपुणता दिखाता है वह इन रिबनों में से रिबन जीत लेता है। गुलिवर डंडों और अपने रूमाल के साथ एक प्रकार का प्लेटफार्म बनाता है। वह घुड़सवारों को इस पर अभ्यास करने के लिए कहता है। सम्राट इसका आनंद लेता है।

गुलिवर की टोपी समुद्र के किनारे मिली

गुलिवर करतब दिखाने में मशगूल था तभी उसे सूचित किया गया कि समुद्र के किनारे एक काले रंग की कोई निर्जीव वस्तु प्राप्त हुई है। गुलिवर ने यह पाया कि ये उसकी टोपी थी जो उसने Antelope (एंटीलोप) जहाज पर यात्रा के दौरान खो दी थी। उस टोपी की दशा बिगड़ चुकी थी परंतु वह अच्छी दिख रही थी। उसने सम्राट से निवेदन किया कि उसे उसकी टोपी दे दी जाए।

Distinction	– उच्च श्रेणी का	Enterprises	– नई योजना, व्यापार आदि उपक्रम
Sublime	– अनंत/विशिष्ट	Presume	– अनुमान लगाना
Meadow	– घास का मैदान	Trample	– कुचलना
Despatch	– संदेश	Solemn	– गंभीर
Malice	– द्वेष	Prostrating	– शालीनता से सिर झुका लेना
Vanity	– घमंड, दंभ	Stipulated	– अनुबंध करना
Oath	– शपथ	Censure	– कटु निंदा करना
Acknowledgements	– आभारोक्ति, स्वीकृति	Peculiar	– विशेष

Important Questions

Questions based on the Plot of the Chapter

Q 1. Describe the diversions in Lilliput.

लिलिपुट राज्य में होने वाले मनोरंजक कार्यक्रमों का वर्णन करें।

लिलिपुटवासियों में कुछ मजाकिया आदतें होना – सम्राट का गुलिवर के लिए कार्यक्रम का आयोजन करना – गुलिवर का लिलिपुटवासियों के रस्सी नृत्य को देखकर खुश हो जाना – आवेदकों को उच्च पदों हेतु रस्सी पर नृत्य करना पड़ता है – बिना गिरे सबसे ज्यादा ऊँचे कूदने वाले को उच्च पद प्रदान किया जाना – दूसरे मनोरंजन में प्रतिभागियों को एक डंडे के ऊपर से कूदने या नीचे से रेंगने को कहा जाना – इसमें सफल होने वालों को क्रमशः नीला, हरा तथा लाल रूमाल दिया जाना – विजेताओं का इन धागों को अपनी कमर पर बाँधना।

Ans. The Lilliputians had some very funny habits and practices. The emperor arranged an entertainment for Gulliver where he was impressed by the skill and dexterity of the Lilliputians.

He was highly impressed with the rope dancing skills of the Lilliputians. Candidates for high posts in the court had to dance on a tight rope and had to prove their superiority in this skill over others in order to get selected.

The one, who jumped the highest without falling, was offered a high post. Often the Chief Ministers were asked to show their skills. Another such activity to contest for high post was either to leap over or to creep under a stick that was held by the emperor.

Those who excelled, were honoured with blue coloured silken thread, the next bagged the green coloured one and the third one had to be satisfied with red coloured thread. The winners wore these threads around their waist as a mark of great honour.

Q 2. Rope dancing was the most dangerous activity. How?

रस्सी नृत्य सर्वाधिक खतरनाक गतिविधि थी। कैसे?

बहुत से कार्यक्रमों द्वारा गुलिवर का मनोरंजन किया जाना – रस्सी नृत्य उन्हीं कार्यक्रमों में से एक होना – उच्च पद हेतु लिलिपुटवासियों का ऐसा नृत्य करने के लिए विवश होना – बहुत से प्रतिभागियों का दुर्घटनाग्रस्त हो जाना – मंत्रियों को अपनी कुशलता और योग्यता दिखाने के दबाव में आकर गिर जाना।

Ans. Gulliver was entertained by many diversions. One of such diversions was rope dancing. The Lilliputians had to walk a tight rope in order to gain promotion at court. The one who jumped the highest without falling, was offered the high office. Often the ministers were asked to show their skills. Sometimes, such displays proved to be fatal. Many candidates met with fatal accidents.

Sometimes, they broke their limbs. But the danger was much greater when the ministers were commanded to show their dexterity. While performing these acts, they strained so much that they would receive a serious fall.

Q 3. What was the black thing that made Gulliver happy?

किस काली वस्तु ने गुलिवर को खुश कर दिया था?

स्वतंत्रता मिलने के पश्चात् गुलिवर का सम्राट तथा उसकी मंत्रिपरिषद् का मनोरंजन करना – समुद्र के पास एक काली वस्तु मिलने की सूचना मिलना – उसकी वस्तु का चारों ओर से फैली हुई तथा बीच में से उठी हुई होना – गुलिवर का उस वस्तु के बारे में जानकर खुश होना – वह वस्तु गुलिवर की टोपी होना।

Ans. After getting liberty, one day Gulliver was entertaining the emperor and his court when they got a news that some of his subjects had seen a great black substance lying on the place where Gulliver was first taken up.

The thing had odd shape, extending from its edges round and rising up in the middle as high as a man. But that thing was not a living creature because it lay on grass without motion. By mounting upon each other's shoulders, they had got to the top, which was flat and even as well as hollow within. They assumed that this thing might belong to the man-mountain. Gulliver was very happy to know about this thing because it was his hat, which he thought, had been lost in the sea.

4

Gulliver Roams Around the City

Gulliver gets his freedom and goes to Mildendo, the capital city of the Lilliputians. All the Lilliputians are told to stay indoors for fear of being crushed to death.

The town is 500 feet square with a wall surrounding it. It can hold 5,00,000 people. The emperor wants Gulliver to see his palace. Gulliver makes a stool for himself to sit to see the things. He carries this stool with him to see the things.

Internal Conflict in Lilliput

Gulliver learns through Reldresal that there are two sources of conflict, internal and external, in Lilliput. The kingdom is divided into two groups-Tramecksan and Slamecksan, constantly fighting with each other. Tramecksan wear high-heeled shoes while Slamecksan low-heeled.

External Conflict in Lilliput

Besides, Lilliput has been at war with Blefuscu for the last three years. Blefuscu is a second island empire, which is equally large and powerful as Lilliput. The islands have been fighting over the issue of how to break an egg. The emperor's grandfather broke the egg on the bigger end and cut his finger in his childhood.

The government of Blefuscu accused the Lilliputians of disobeying their religion's principle. It was called 'Brundrecral' by breaking their eggs at the small end first.

4

गुलिवर ने शहर का भ्रमण किया

Gulliver (गुलिवर) को स्वतंत्रता मिल जाती है और वह लिलिपुट की राजधानी Mildendo (मिलडेंडो) चला जाता है। सभी लिलिपुटवासियों को कुचलकर मर जाने के भय से अंदर रुकने के लिए कहा जाता है।

शहर उसके चारों तरफ एक दीवार के साथ 500 फुट वर्गाकार है। इसमें 5,00,000 व्यक्ति आ सकते हैं। सम्राट चाहता है कि गुलिवर उसके महल को देखे। गुलिवर बैठकर चीजें देखने के लिए अपने लिए एक स्टूल बनाता है। वह चीजें देखने के लिए इस स्टूल को अपने साथ ले जाता है।

लिलिपुट में आंतरिक मतभेद

Reldresal (रेल्ड्रेसल) ने गुलिवर को बताया था कि लिलिपुट में मतभेद एवं संघर्ष के दो मुख्य कारण थे–आंतरिक एवं बाह्य। राज्य भी दो भागों में बँटा हुआ है Tramecksan (ट्रेमेक्सन) एवं Slamecksan (स्लेमेक्सन) एवं इन दोनों दलों में परस्पर मतभेद जारी रहते थे। ट्रेमेक्सन दल के समर्थक ऊँची एड़ी वाले जूते पहनते थे, परंतु इसके विपरीत स्लेमेक्सन दल के समर्थक नीची एड़ी वाले जूते पहनते थे।

लिलिपुट में बाह्य मतभेद

इसके अतिरिक्त लिलिपुट राज्य की Blefuscu (ब्लेफुस्कु) राज्य के साथ पिछले तीन वर्षों से लड़ाई चल रही थी। ब्लेफुस्कु एक दूसरा द्वीपीय साम्राज्य था जिसकी क्षमता एवं ताकत लिलिपुट के बराबर थी। इन दोनों राज्यों के मध्य झगड़ा होने की मुख्य वजह थी कि अंडे को किस प्रकार तोड़ा जाए। सम्राट के दादा ने अंडे को बड़े वाले सिरे की तरफ से तोड़ा था तथा उनकी अँगुली इस प्रयास में कट गई थी।

ब्लेफुस्कु की सरकार ने लिलिपुटवासियों को धार्मिक Principle (सिद्धांत) को न मानने का दोषी माना। उनके अंडों को पहले छोटे आकार में तोड़ने को Brundrecral कहा जाता था।

Word Meaning

Metropolis	– बड़ा शहर	Encompassed	– सम्मिलित था
Flanked	– चारों ओर से घिरा	Eaves	– छत की जगह
Peril	– खतरा	Hewn	– अनियमित आकार का
Hooked	– मुड़ी हुई	Contrivance	– उपकरण, विधि
Anticipate	– अनुमान लगाना	Solicitations	– याचिका या प्रार्थना-पत्र
Animosities	– दुश्मनी	Hobble	– लंगड़ाना
Disquiets	– अशांति	Gait	– चाल
Primitive	– आदिम, आदिकालीन	Resented	– नापसंद करना
Fomented	– उकसाना	Quelled	– कुचल दिया गया
Expostulate	– झगड़ा, बहस	schism	– फूट, विच्छेद
Reckoned	– समझना	Hazard	– जोखिम
Faction	– विरोध, बलवा	Circumspection	– सावधानीपूर्वक
Straggler	– धीमे चलने वाली गाड़ी		

Important Questions

Questions based on the Plot of the Chapter

Q 1. Describe the city of Mildendo—the Metropolis in detail.

मिलडेंडो शहर का विस्तार से वर्णन करें।

गुलिवर को अपनी स्वतंत्रता मिल जाती है – सम्राट से मिलडेंडो शहर देखने की आज्ञा माँगता है – आज्ञा दे दी जाती है – सख्त निर्देश दिए जाते हैं कि वह किसी भी व्यक्ति अथवा किसी घर को कोई नुकसान नहीं पहुँचाएगा – मिलडेंडों एक घनी आबादी वाला शहर है – शहर में 5,00,000 लोग रह सकते हैं – बहुमंजली इमारतों में रहते हैं – शहर के चारों ओर ढाई फुट ऊँची दीवार है – सम्राट का महल शहर के बीचोबीच स्थित है – गुलिवर शहर की भव्यता देखकर बहुत प्रभावित होता है।

Ans. Gulliver got his freedom and he expressed his desire to see Mildendo—the metropolis. The permission was granted with the strict instruction not to harm either the inhabitants or their houses. Hence, Gulliver wore his short waistcoat as the skirts of his longer garments would damage the roofs and eaves of the houses.

Milendo was a thickly populated city. The whole city, an exact square, was divided into four equal squares by two great streets.

The city could accommodate 5,00,000 people who lived in multi-storeyed houses. The whole city was surrounded by a two and a half foot high wall which was about eleven inches broad so that a coach and horses could be driven on it.

The lane and alleys were twelve to eighteen inches wide. The emperor's palace was in the centre of the city where the two great streets met. Gulliver was very impressed with its magnificence.

Q 2. Describe the internal conflict in Lilliput.

लिलिपुट की आंतरिक कलह का वर्णन करें।

राज्य का मुख्य सचिव रेल्ड्रेसल गुलिवर से मिलने आया – उसने गुलिवर को लिलिपुट की समस्याओं के बारे में विस्तार से बताया, जिसमें आंतरिक कलह तथा बाहरी संघर्ष दोनों ही सम्मिलित थे – आंतरिक कलह का कारण दो दलों–ट्रेमेक्सन (ऊँची एड़ी) तथा स्लेमेक्सन (छोटी एड़ी) के मध्य का द्वंद्व था – लिलिपुट के प्राचीन काल में ट्रेमेक्सन का शासन था – अब सम्राट केवल स्लेमेक्सन के लोगों को ही प्रशासनिक सेवा में नियुक्त करता था – दोनों के मध्य इस बात को लेकर द्वंद्व था – ट्रेमेक्सन की संख्या अधिक थी, किंतु सत्ता स्लेमेक्सन के हाथों में थी – राजा अभी यह निश्चय नहीं कर पाया कि वह किस प्रकार के जूते पहने – वह ऊँची एड़ी तथा छोटी एड़ी दोनों प्रकार के जूते पहनता था।

Ans. After a fortnight, Reldresal, the Principal Secretary of Private Affairs come to Gulliver's house and informed him about the two major problems of Lillputians—one was an internal conflict and the other was a danger of foreign invasion. The internal conflict was the result of the friction between the two parties.

Tramecksan and Slamecksan, from the high and low heels of their shoes. They distinguished themselves by this. The high heels (Tramecksan) were most agreeable to their ancient constitution but the emperor made use only of low heels (Slamecksan) in the administration of the government. The emperor himself was of low heels. This difference in treatment had caused conflict between these two parties.

The hostilities between these parties was so high, that they would neither eat nor drink, nor talk with each other. The Tramecksan or high heels were more in number but the power was wholly in the hands of Slamecksan. But, the emperor had a soft corner for high heels so one of his heels was higher than the other, which gave him a hobble in his walk.

Gulliver Prevents the Blefuscu Invasion

Gulliver devises a plan to serve Lilliput after spying on Blefuscu. He makes hooks with cable attached. He then catches their ships after swimming the channel to Blefuscu.

The Blefuscu soldiers are greatly frightened and fire arrows at him. He protects his eyes by wearing spectacles which he keeps in his coat pocket.

Gulliver's Refusal to Enslave the Blefuscudians— A Beginning of Conspiracy

He is asked by the emperor to destroy the Blefuscu's military and naval power. He also asks him to make Blefuscu, a part of Lilliput, but Gulliver asks him not to do that. It will mean encouraging slavery and injustice. The officials in the government oppose Gulliver for it and want to kill him.

Peace Treaty Offered by Blefuscu

About three weeks after Gulliver captures the Blefuscu fleet, Blefuscu's emperor sends a group ambassadors asking for a peace treaty with Lilliput. The emperor of Lilliput agrees with the treaty but on certain conditions favourable to him.

Gulliver is also invited to come and visit Blefuscu. Gulliver asks for the emperor's permission to go to Blefuscu. The emperor agrees, but unhappily

5

गुलिवर ने ब्लेफुस्कु आक्रमण से बचाव किया

Blefuscu (ब्लेफुस्कु) के ऊपर जासूसी के पश्चात् Gulliver (गुलिवर) Lilliput (लिलिपुट) की सेवा करने की योजना बनाता है। वह केबल जोड़ने के साथ हुक बनाता है। फिर वह उनके पोतों को ब्लेफुस्कु चैनल में तैरकर पकड़ लेता है।

ब्लेफुस्कु के सैनिक काफी भयभीत हो जाते हैं और उस पर तीर चलाते हैं वह अपनी आँखों को चश्में के साथ बचाता है। जिन्हें वह अपने कोट की जेब में रखता है।

गुलिवर का ब्लेफुस्कु सैनिकों को बंदी बनाने से इंकार-षड्यंत्र की शुरूआत

सम्राट द्वारा उसे ब्लेफुस्कु की Military (मिलिट्री) और Naval (नौसेना) की ताकत का विनाश करने के लिए कहा जाता है। वह उसे ब्लेफुस्कु को लिलिपुट का हिस्सा बनाने के लिए कहता है, परंतु गुलिवर उसे ऐसा न करने के लिए कहता है। इसका मतलब दासता और अन्याय को उत्साहित करना होगा। सरकार के कुछ कर्मचारी इसके लिए गुलिवर का विरोध करते हैं और उसे मारना चाहते हैं।

ब्लेफुस्कु द्वारा शांति प्रस्ताव

ब्लेफुस्कु के जहाजी बेड़े को पकड़ने के तीन सप्ताह बाद गुलिवर को लिलिपुट राज्य के साथ शांति संधि के प्रस्ताव का समाचार मिला जो ब्लेफुस्कु के सम्राट ने भेजा था। लिलिपुट के सम्राट ने कुछ शर्तों के साथ इस संधि प्रस्ताव को स्वीकार करने का निर्णय ले लिया।

गुलिवर को ब्लेफुस्कु राज्य में आने का निमंत्रण दिया। गुलिवर ने सम्राट से ब्लेफुस्कु राज्य तक जाने की अनुमति माँगी। सम्राट ने उसे अनुमति दे दी, परंतु वह प्रसन्न नहीं था।

Word Meaning

Channel	– पानी के रास्ते का गहरा भाग	Embargo	– पाबंदी, निषेध
Plumbed	– नलकार की भाँति कार्य	Glumgluffs	– छः फुट के बराबर
Hillock	– छोटी पहाड़ी	Trebled	– किसी वस्तु का तिगुना हो जाना
Tackling	– उपकरण	Prow	– जहाज का सबसे आगे का भाग
Adrift	– बिना किसी लक्ष्य के	Nardac	– एक उपाधि
Discern	– कठिनाई से किसी वस्तु को देख या पहचान पाना	Hostile	– व्यक्ति या वस्तु के प्रति अत्यंत उग्र भावनाओं वाला
Encomiums	– प्रशंसा, स्तुति	Junta	– समूह
Gratify	– संतोष रखना	Whisper	– धीमे स्वर में फुसफुसाना
Disaffection	– लगाव का अभाव होना	Antiquity	– प्राचीनकालिक
Credentials	– व्यक्ति के गुण या प्रत्यय पत्र	Intercourse	– आदान-प्रदान
Gentry	– सभ्य व सुसंस्कृत लोग	Maritime	– समुद्र या जहाजों से संबंधित
Servile	– दासता में होना	Incessantly	– लगातार, बिना रुके
Thimble	– धातु की बनी छोटी टोपी	Stifled	– दमघोटू
Deplorable	– शोचनीय, निंदनीय	Abhorrence	– घृणा की प्रबल भावना
Confidents	– गहरे मित्र या कर्मचारी		

Important Questions

Questions based on the Plot of the Chapter

Q 1. How does Gulliver succeed to prevent the invasion of Blefuscu? Explain.

गुलिवर ब्लेफुस्कु के हमले को रोकने में कैसे सफल होता है? व्याख्या करें।

ब्लेफुस्कु तथा लिलिपुट के मध्य एक गहरा समुद्री रास्ता है – गुलिवर ब्लेफुस्कु के जहाजी बेड़े को रोकने की योजना बनाता है – वह केबल तथा लोहे की छड़ों से बने हुक को जोड़ता है – वह ब्लेफुस्कु के बेड़े तक तैरकर पहुँच जाता है – ब्लेफुस्कु के सैनिक भयभीत हो जाते हैं – उस पर तीर चलाते हैं – वह आँखों को चश्में के साथ बचाता है – वह जहाजी बेड़े के एंकर को काट देता है – प्रत्येक जहाज को हुक से बाँध देता है – सभी केबल को एक साथ बाँधकर जहाजी बेड़े को लिलिपुट की ओर खींच लेता है – लिलिपुट का सम्राट तथा निवासी बहुत खुश होते हैं – उसे लिलिपुट राज्य की सर्वोच्च उपाधि प्रदान करता है।

Ans. Blefuscu and Lilliput were seperated by a channel which was 800 yards wide and six feet deep. Gulliver told the emperor that he would seize the whole fleet of ships of his enemy. He took a few cables and a large number of iron bars. By twisting three bars together, he bent them into hook like shapes and tied these hooks to those cables. He waded through the channel, carrying those cables and hooks. When the soldiers of Blefuscu saw this man-mountain, they panicked and ran to save their lives. Gulliver then fastened the hooks to each of the ships of Blefuscu. He tied all the cables together.

Meanwhile, he was attacked by the soldiers of Blefuscu and he saved himself by wearing spectacles on his eyes. He cut the cables of all the anchored ships and pulled the whole fleet of fifty ships. Wading and swimming through the channel, he carried the fleet to Lilliput. It was a great blow to Blefuscu. The emperor of Lilliput and its people were highly dilighted, Gulliver had successfully accomplished this great mission of humbling the enemy and thwarting the intended invasion. For this, the emperor of Lilliput conferred on Gulliver the highest title of honour which existed in Lilliput.

Q 2. Gulliver succeeds to prevent the Blefuscudian invasion and is conferred on a title by the emperor, yet the emperor is so angry with him that he designs a plot to kill him. Explain.

गुलिवर ब्लेफुस्कु के हमले को नाकाम करता है तथा राजा उसे एक उपाधि प्रदान करता है, तब भी सम्राट उससे इतना नाराज होता है कि उसे मारने की योजना बनाता है। समझाएँ।

गुलिवर लिलिपुट को ब्लेफुस्कु के आक्रमण से बचाता है – किंतु सम्राट ब्लेफुस्कु राज्य को पूरी तरह से पराजित करना चाहता था – वह वायसराय की सहायता से ब्लेफुस्कु पर राज करना चाहता था, लेकिन गुलिवर इस प्रकार ब्लेफुस्कु राज्य को नुकसान नहीं पहुँचाना चाहता – न ही अकारण खून-खराबा करना चाहता था – वह सम्राट की आशाओं को झुठला देता है – सम्राट उसके प्रति उदासीन हो जाता है – फिल्मनैप और बोलगोलाम गुलिवर के विरुद्ध सम्राट के कान भरते हैं – वे सम्राट को विश्वास दिला देते हैं कि गुलिवर का ब्लेफुस्कु राज्य के प्रति दोस्ती का तात्पर्य लिलिपुट के विरुद्ध होना है – दूसरी ओर रानी भी गुलिवर से नाराज हो जाती है क्योंकि वह शाही महल में लगी आग को मूत्र विसर्जन द्वारा बुझाता है – महल के दरबारियों के षड्यंत्र के कारण सम्राट गुलिवर के विरुद्ध हो जाता है – उसे मारने की योजना बनाता है।

Ans. Lilliput was saved by Gulliver. Blefuscu fleet was captured and destroyed. The emperor of Lilliput wanted to demolish and damage the armed forces of Blefuscu completely. He wanted to rule over Blefuscu through a viceroy. But Gulliver was not in favour of causing so much harm to Blefuscu.

He didn't believe in causing unnecessary bloodshed and damage to the enemy. He fulfilled the expectations of the emperor. So the emperor became cool towards Gulliver. Soon Flimnap and Bolgolam were able to prejudice the emperor against Gulliver. They convinced that Gulliver's withdrawl of support to Lilliput means his friendliness with Blefuscu. On the other hand, the queen was also annoyed because Gulliver urinated to extinguish the fire of her palace. Being victim of some consipiracy by some of the courtiers, he was to be trialled. Filmnap poisoned the ears of the emperor against Gulliver. So he started designing a plot to kill him.

Q 3. Gulliver saves the royal palace from destruction. The empress is highly offended. Is Gulliver justified in his act? Why/Why not? Justify your answer.

गुलिवर शाही महल को नष्ट होने से बचाता है। रानी अत्यधिक अपमानित महसूस करती है। क्या गुलिवर अपने इस कार्य में न्यायसंगत है? क्यों/क्यों नहीं? तर्कसंगत उत्तर दें।

एक रात शाही महल में आग लग जाती है गुलिवर को मदद के लिए बुलाया जाता है – गुलिवर उस आग को अपने मूत्र से बुझाता है – गुलिवर का यह कृत्य न्यायसंगत है – उसने यह कार्य रानी की जान बचाने के लिए किया है – हालाँकि वह अपने कोट द्वारा भी आग बुझा सकता था – लेकिन वह उसे घर पर ही छोड़ आता है – आग की लपटें इतनी तेज हैं कि कुछ ही देर में वह भव्य महल राख बन जाता – पानी पर्याप्त मात्रा में उपलब्ध नहीं है – अत: उसके पास यही एक उपाय बचता है – जिसके कारण वह रानी की जान बचा पाता है।

Ans. One night, Gulliver was alarmed at the shouting of the Lilliputians. The palace of Imperial majesty caught fire. Water could not be accessed to extinguish it.

The Lilliputians urged the 'man-mountain' Gulliver to help them to come out of this problem. Gulliver's coat could have become handy at this situation, but he had left it in the room. Then an idea stuck him and he 'made water' on the palace to put out the fire. The emperor was pleased, but the empress got annoyed with this illegals act and refused to live in that palace.

His act was very much justified because whatever he did, he did it to save the life of the empress. At that moment, he had no option but to urinate on the fire. There was not sufficient amount of water.

He could have easily stifled those violent flames of fire with his coat but unfortunately he left it in his house. If he had not urinated, the magnificient palace would have been burnt down to the ground. So with the presence of his mind, he was able to save the life of the empress.

Questions based on the Character Sketch

Q 4. The emperor of Lilliput wants to enslave Blefuscu. He also designs a plot to kill Gulliver. What qualities of his character are highlighted therby? Explain.

लिलिपुट का सम्राट ब्लेफुस्कु पर कब्जा करना चाहता है। वह गुलिवर को मारने की भी योजना बनाता है। इससे उसके चरित्र के किन गुणों के बारे में पता चलता है? समझाएँ।

गुलिवर ब्लेफुस्कु आक्रमण को सफलतापूर्वक निष्क्रिय कर देता है – राजा इससे संतुष्ट नहीं होता है – उसका यह विचार उसकी सत्ता की भूख को दर्शाता है – इससे उसकी संकीर्ण मानसिकता, स्वार्थपरकता तथा छोटेपन का पता चलता है। लिलिपुट का सम्राट एक निरंकुश शासक है – जब गुलिवर ब्लेफुस्कु सेना को तबाह करने से मना कर देता है – वह गुलिवर के प्रति उदासीन हो जाता है।

Ans. Gulliver had successfully spoiled the invasion of Blefuscu on Lilliput. He drowned their fleet of fifty ships into Lilliputian port. The emperor was not satisfied by this, he wanted him to totally shatter the empire of Blefuscu by bringing all the rest of their ships to Lilliput. This proposal was thoroughly unjustified and prompted by his ambition and lust for power. His act highlighted his shallowness, meanness and pettiness. The emperor was first and foremost a despot. He could not digest that any man may disobey or ignore his directives and suggestions. He wanted to rule unchallenged.

When Gulliver refrained from destroying Blefuscu's army, he could not tolerate it. He grew cool towards him and even indirectly supported the conspirators against Gulliver by not checking their moves. This showed his ingratitude towards all the acts of Gulliver which he had done for the betterment of Lilliputians.

Introduction

In this chapter, Gulliver describes some customs and traditions of Lilliput, including animal, trees and plants. The size of these is in proportion to the people. The Lilliputions can see very clearly but Gulliver can't. They are well educated, though Gulliver finds it difficult to under their writing system.

परिचय

इस पाठ में Lilliput (लिलिपुट) की कुछ Customs (रीति-रिवाजों), जानवरों वृक्षों के बारे में वर्णन करता है। इनका आकार व्यक्तियों के अनुसार है। लिलिपुटवासी बहुत साफ देखते हैं परंतु गुलिवर नहीं देख सकता। वे अत्यधिक पढ़े-लिखे हैं यद्यपि उनके लिखने के सिस्टम को समझने में गुलिवर कठिनाई पाता है।

Customs

The Lilliputians bury their dead with their heads pointing directly downward. They do so as they believe that the dead will rise again and that the earth will turn upside down. Gulliver states that the educated don't believe in these customs.

Gulliver states that there tradition in Lilliput. It is that anyone who falsely accuses some one of a crime against the state will be put to death.

रीति-रिवाज

Lilliputians (लिलिपुटवासी) अपने मृत को उनके सिरों को सीधे नीचे की तरफ रखकर दफनाते हैं। वे ऐसा इसलिए करते हैं क्योंकि वे विश्वास करते हैं कि मृत पुन: जीवित हो जाएँगे और धरती ऊपर से नीचे हो जाएगी। गुलिवर कहता है कि शिक्षित इन रीति-रिवाजों में विश्वास नहीं करते।

Gulliver (गुलिवर) बताता है कि लिलिपुट में एक रिवाज है। जो कोई दूसरे राष्ट्र के विरुद्ध का झूठा अपराध लगाता है उसे फाँसी की सजा दी जाएगी।

Word Meaning

Treatise	– प्रबंध	Geese	– बत्तख जैसे सफेद पक्षी, जिन्हें मांस के लिए पाला जाता है।
Gradations	– सोपानें		
Resurrection	– पुन: जीवन	Absurdity	– बेतुकापन, असंगत बात
Compliance	– अनुपालन, अनुरूपता	Ignominious	– तिरस्कृत, अपयशी
Perpetual	– चिरस्थायी	Connived	– गलत काम की अनदेखी करना
Interceding	– तोल-मोल करना	Extenuation	– घटाव
Hinges	– सन्धि	Providence	– दूरदर्शिता
Temp erance	– नियंत्रण	Weal	– घाव
Scandalons	– कलंक लगाने वाला	Corruption	– भ्रष्टाचार

Important Questions

Questions based on the Plot of the Chapter

Q 1. Describe those customs appearing strange and absurd, in detail.

बेतुके व अजीव रीति-रिवाजों को विस्तार से समझाएँ।

लिलिपुटवासियों के कुछ रीति-रिवाज अजीब व हास्यास्पद थे – वे लोग कागज के एक कोने से दूसरे कोने तक तिरछा लिखते थे – वे अपने मृतकों को सिर नीचे की ओर दफनाते थे – उनका मानना था कि एक दिन धरती पलट जाएगी – तब उनके ये मृतक पुनर्जीवित हो जाएँगें व अपने पैरों पर खड़े होंगें – वे बच्चों के ऊपर माता-पिता के प्रति कोई कर्त्तव्य नहीं मानते थे – बच्चे राष्ट्र द्वारा न कि माता-पिता द्वारा पाले-पोसे जाते थे – उनकी शिक्षा का भार भी राष्ट्र द्वारा वहन किया जाता था।

Ans. Lilliputians followed some customs which were very absurd and strange. They had a peculiar style of writing. They wrote from one corner of the page to the other, diagonally across the page. They buried their dead upside down as they beleved that after eleven thousand moon, the earth (which they conceived to be slat) would turn upside down, at their resurrection, making them stand on their feet, Though the learned saw no logic in this belief, this practice still persisted. The concept of filial gratitude was absent among Lilliputian. They didn't feel that a child should feel grateful to the parents for beringing him into this world. The parents were not entrusted with the education of the child. Therefore, they had public nurseries, where parents were obliged to send their infants. In this way, Lilliputians had some very strang and irrelevent customs.

Articles of Impeachment Issued

Gulliver describes the plot that results in his departure from Lilliput. He prepares to make a trip of Blefuscu. But a government official informs Gulliver that he has been charged with treason by the enemies in the government. He shows Gulliver the document that he is to be put to death for that. The charges against Gulliver are he has urinated in the public, he has refused to obey the emperor to seize the remaining Blefuscu ships, etc.

गुलिवर पर महाभियोग के आरोप निश्चित हो गए

Gulliver (गुलिवर) उस षड्यंत्र का वर्णन करता है जिसका परिणाम उसके Lilliput (लिलिपुट) से चले जाने में होता है। वह Blefuscu (ब्लेफुस्कु) में जाने की तैयारी करता है परंतु अदालत का एक कर्मचारी गुलिवर को बताता है कि सरकार ने दुश्मनों द्वारा उस पर देशद्रोह का आरोप लगाया है। वह गुलिवर को कागज दिखाता है कि उसके लिए उसे फाँसी की सजा दी जानी है। गुलिवर के विरुद्ध आरोप है कि उसने पब्लिक में Urinate (पेशाब) किया है, उसने बचे हुए ब्लेफुस्कु पोतों पर कब्जा करने के सम्राट के आदेशों को न मानने से इंकार किया है आदि।

Punishments Suggested for Gulliver

The official informs Gulliver that Reldresal pleaded for the reduction of his sentence. He called not for execution but for putting his eyes out. This punishment has been agreed upon together with starving him to death. His eyes will be put out in three days. Gulliver fears this operation. He crosses the channel and arrives in Blefuscu.

गुलिवर के लिए सजा प्रस्तावित की गई

कर्मचारी गुलिवर को बताता है कि Reldresal (रेल्ड्रेसल) ने उसकी सजा कम करने की प्रार्थना की है। उसने उसे फाँसी न देने परंतु उसकी आँखें निकालने के लिए कहा था। उसे इस सजा पर और साथ-साथ भूखा मारने पर सहमति हो गई है। उसकी आँखें तीन दिन में निकाल ली जाएँगी। गुलिवर इस सजा से डर जाता है। वह नदी पार करता है और ब्लेफुस्कु पहुँच जाता है।

Word Meaning

Intrigue	– षड्यंत्र रचना	Remote	– अलग, दूर का
Admittance	– प्रवेश की आज्ञा	Salutations	– अभिवादन शब्द
Conjunction	– संयोग से	Notorious	– बदनाम, कुख्यात
Chamberlain	– राजमहल का अधिकारी	Impeachment	– महाभियोग, अविश्वास
Procured	– उपलब्ध करना, प्राप्त करना	Venture	– करने का साहस करना

Important Questions

Questions based on the Plot of the Chapter

Q 1. What were the articles of impeachment issued against Gulliver? Explain in detail.

गुलिवर के विरुद्ध लगाए गए महाभियोग के आरोप क्या थे? विस्तार से वर्णन करें।

विद्वेषी व ईर्ष्यालु दरबारियों ने गुलिवर के विरुद्ध षड्यंत्र करके सम्राट के कान भर दिए – उसके विरुद्ध राष्ट्रद्रोह तथा अन्य मुख्य अपराधों का आरोप लगाया – महाभियोग के आरोपों की सूची बनाई गई – उसमें पहला आरोप उसके देशद्रोही होने का लगाया गया – क्योंकि उसने शाही महल की आग को पानी उत्पन्न (मूत्र विसर्जन) करके बुझाया था – उसका यह अपराध और अधिक गंभीर हो गया जब उसके सम्राट की लिखित अनुमति के बिना ही ब्लेफुस्कु जाने का निश्चय किया – इसके अतिरिक्त, उसके कई छोटे अपराधों को भी सूचीबद्ध किया गया था।

Ans. The malicious and vindictive courtiers conspired against Gulliver and poisoned the emperor's ears against him and charged him for treason and other capital crime. The articles of impeachment were prepared against Gulliver. There were many charges against him. The first article accused him of treason as he had made water (urinated) in princincts of the royal palace while extinguishing the fire of the empress' palace. The second article accused him as a traitor because he had refused to obey the emperor when he had been ordered to seize all the ships of Blefuscu and to help him destroy all the Big-Endians.

He was also accused of showing courtesy and hospitality to Blefuscuian ambassadors. His crimes were termed more serious as he intended to visit Blefuscu without taking written permission of the emperor. Apart from it, some minor charges were also listed. These conspirators tried their utmost to get Gulliver sentenced to death by imperial orders.

Introduction

After three days Gulliver sees a boat of normal size. He finds it overturned in the water. It is of his size. He asks the emperor of Blefuscu to set the boat right. Meanwhile, the emperor of Lilliput sends an ambassador to Blefuscu with the order that Gulliver should give up his eyesight. The emperor of Blefuscu sends the ambassador back stating that Gulliver would soon leave both the kingdoms. Gulliver sets the boats right after about a month and is ready to sail. He arrives safely back in England. He makes a good profit in showing the miniature farm animals that he took with him from Blefuscu.

परिचय

तीन दिन के पश्चात् Gulliver (गुलिवर) एक सामान्य आकार की नौका देखता है। वह इसे पानी में उल्टी पड़ी हुई पाता है। यह उसके आकार की है। वह Blefuscu (ब्लेफुस्कु) के सम्राट को इस नौका को ठीक कराने के लिए कहता है। इसी बीच में Lilliput (लिलिपुट) का सम्राट ब्लेफुस्कु में एक राजदूत इस आदेश के साथ भेजता है कि गुलिवर को अपनी आँखें निकाल देनी चाहिए। ब्लेफुस्कु का सम्राट उस राजदूत को यह कहकर वापस भेज देता है कि गुलिवर शीघ्र ही इस राज्य को छोड़ देगा। गुलिवर लगभग एक महीने पश्चात् नौका को ठीक कर लेता है और समुद्री यात्रा के लिए तैयार होता है। वह सुरक्षापूर्वक England (इंग्लैंड) में वापस पहुँच जाता है। वह ब्लेफुस्कु में जानवरों के छोटे-छोटे फार्म दिखाने में अत्यधिक Profit (लाभ) कमाता है, जिन्हें वह ब्लेफुस्कु से लाया था।

Word Meaning

Tempest	– भयानक तूफान	Cordage	– जहाज की रस्सियाँ
Shove	– धकेलना	Stowed	– सुरक्षित रूप से छिपाना
Concourse	– समूह या झुंड	Prodigious	– विशालकाय, भयंकर, अनिष्टसूचक
Expostulations	– तर्क करना	Cabal	– गुप्त दल, राजनीतिज्ञ षड्यंत्र
Envoy	– संदेशवाहक	Amity	– मित्रता
Encumbrance	– भार	Tallow	– चर्बी

Important Questions

Questions based on the Plot of the Chapter

Q 1. Describe his departure from Blefuscu.

गुलिवर का ब्लेफुस्कु से प्रस्थान का वर्णन करें।

ब्लेफुस्कु पहुँचने के तीन दिन बाद उसे समुद्र में एक उल्टी नौका दिखाई देती है – सम्राट की आज्ञा से गुलिवर उसकी मरम्मत करता है ताकि वह उस पर वापस इंग्लैंड जा सके – सम्राट द्वारा अनुमति मिलने पर गुलिवर अपने घर जाने की तैयारी करता है – सम्राट उसे एक भावपूर्ण विदाई देता है – उसे बहुत से सोने के सिक्के व अपना चित्र उपहार स्वरूप भेंट करता है – गुलिवर भोजन के लिए अपनी नौका को बहुत से बैल, भेड़ों, गाय के शवों से भर लेता है – वह कुछ जानवरों को अपने साथ इंग्लैंड ले जाना चाहता है – अपने साथ वह उन पशुओं के लिए चारा व मक्का भी रखता है – इस प्रकार पूरी तैयारी के बाद वह अपनी यात्रा प्रारंभ करता है।

Ans. Three days after his arrival in Blefuscu, Gulliver found an upturned boat in the sea. It was a boat of normal size which could carry Gulliver away in the sea. The emperor of Blefuscu allowed fitting the boat for a voyage. Gulliver also obtained his permission to venture to leave for his native country. The emperor declined the request of Lilliputian emperor to send this 'trailor' back. So, Gulliver decided to leave Blefuscu for home.

On the day of his departure, the emperor and the royal family came out of their palace to bid farewell to Gulliver. The emperor gifted him with a large number of gold coins and his own picture of full length. Gulliver had filled his boat with a large number of the carcases of oxen, sheep, cows, bulls, etc. To serve as food for him during the voyage.

He wanted to take some of the animals to England to breed such pigmies there. He also took some bundles of hay and a bag of corn to feed those animals. Having thus prepared all things, he set sail to England.

Part II 1

Problems During the Second Voyage

Gulliver stays in England for ten months and again is overpowered by his desire for voyage. He sets on his second voyage on June 20, 1702, on the ship named Adventure, with Captain John Nicholas. It takes one year to reach Madagascar in Africa where they face a violent storm. Besides, they have no water to drink. This reminds us of a line in 'Ancient Mariner' by Coleridge, "Water, water, everywhere, but not a drop to drink...". On June 16, 1703, a boy on the ship noticed an unknown land from the top most.

द्वितीय समुद्री यात्रा के दौरान समस्याएँ

Gulliver (गुलिवर) England (इंग्लैंड) में लगभग दस महीने तक रहा एवं पुन: उसे समुद्री यात्रा पर जाने की इच्छा हुई। वह 20 जून, 1702 को Captain John Nicholas (कप्तान जॉन निकोलस) के साथ Adventure (एडवेंचर) नामक जहाज पर अपनी द्वितीय समुद्री यात्रा पर गया। अफ्रीका में Madagascar (मेडागास्कर) पहुँचने में उसे एक वर्ष लगा, जहाँ उन्होंने एक भयानक तूफान का सामना किया। उनके पास पीने के लिए पानी भी नहीं था। Coleridge (कॉलरिज) द्वारा लिखित Ancient Mariner ('एंसियेंट मारिनर') की पंक्तियों ''हर तरफ पानी ही पानी पर पीने को पानी की एक बूँद नहीं'' की याद दिलाता है। 16 जून, 1703 को एक लड़के ने जहाज के ऊपरी सिरे से देखा तो उसे एक अनजान द्वीप नजर आया।

Gulliver's Encounter with the Huge Giant

As Gulliver is trying to cross the fence, he sees a giant approaching. Gulliver is so afraid that he falls on the ground, remembers his family and the Lilliputians for whom he was man-mountain, but now a number of man-mountains are in front of him.

एक विशालकाय दैत्य से गुलिवर का सामना

जब गुलिवर दीवार फाँदकर भागने का प्रयत्न कर रहा था तभी उसे एक विशालकाय दैत्य नजर आया। गुलिवर डरकर भूमि पर गिर पड़ा, अपने परिवार को तथा लिलिपुटवासियों को याद करने लगा। जिनके लिए वह मानव-पर्वत था, परंतु अब उसके समक्ष बहुत सारे Man-Mountain (मानव-पर्वत) थे।

Word Meaning

Gale	– तेज हवाएँ	Wintered	– सर्दी का मौसम बिताना
Ague	– बुखार का एक दौरा	Rejoiced	– खुशी मनाना
Helm	– जहाज का पहिया	Staunch	– मजबूत
Creek	– झील या नदी की निकासी	Halloo	– चिल्लाना

Important Questions

Questions based on the Plot of the Chapter

Q 1. Describe the storm and the hurdles that Gulliver faced along with his crew, during his second voyage on the Adventure.

दूसरी समुद्री यात्रा के दौरान गुलिवर ने अपने नाविकों के साथ, समुद्री तूफान तथा अन्य परेशानियों या रुकावटों का सामना किया, उसका वर्णन करें।

20 जून, 1702 को गुलिवर पुनः समुद्री यात्रा पर निकला-सूरत जाते समय केप ऑफ गुड होप तक जहाज का सफर सुखद था – वहाँ वे ताजे पानी के लिए उतरे – जहाज में दरार पाई अतः जाड़े के मौसम तक वे वहीं रुके – जहाज का कैप्टन बीमार हो गया – अतः मार्च तक वे वहीं रहे-पुनः यात्रा शुरू की – मेडागास्कर पार किया मेडागास्कर के उत्तरी भाग में वे उस स्थान पर पहुँचे जो बहुत खतरनाक व डरावना था – वह तूफान में घिर गए जो मोलाका द्वीप पूर्वी दिशा में ले गया – 2 मई तक समुद्र शांत रहा – दक्षिणी मानसून में फँस गए – वह एक तेज व खतरनाक तूफान था।

Ans. Gulliver left his native country again on June 20,1702 to sail with the ship Adventure, whose captain was John Nicholas. The ship was bound for Surat and they had a good wind till they arrived at the cape of Good Hope where they anchored for fresh water. There, they discovered a leak in the ship, so they stayed there during the winter and the captain fell sick. Due to these hurdles, they could not leave till the end of March. They then set sail again till they passed the Straits Of Madagascar. But when they got Northwards of the straits, they entered the area which was very rough and dangerous from December to May. Then they were hit by a storm which drifted them to East of the Molucca island. By the end of May, the sea was calm again. The next day, they were caught by the Southern monsoon. It was a very strong and rough storm, but the ship held fast. The only damage was to the sail which split into two. This fierce storm drifted their course altogether. Their supply of fresh water was running out slowly.

Introduction

Gulliver is in Brobdingnag where the people and the animals are having prodigious size. He is caught by a farmer who takes him home and his wife treats him kindly. In the current chapter, Gulliver provides an account of the farmer's daughter who cares for him as long as he is in Brobdingnag.

We learn how he is taken to a market-town and then to the metropolis for diversion of the people and how the farmer makes money by constant stage shows not withstanding Gulliver's weariness and vexation.

Glumdalclitch, the Farmer's Daughter

The farmer's wife has a nine year old daughter, expert in sewing. She sews some clothes for Gulliver. She also teaches Gulliver the mother tongue of Brobdingnag. She fits the baby's cradle as his bed. Gulliver names her 'Glumdalclitch'.

Gulliver Performs Stage Shows

Gulliver is carried in a box to the market-town. He is placed on a table in the largest room in the inn. Glumdalclitch was sitting nearby. Not more than thirty people are allowed to watch him.

The farmer does earn a lavish amount and now he takes Gulliver repeatedly to the market-town and the metropolis. His little nurse, Glumdalclitch always accompanies him. She is very well aware of Gulliver's fatigue and so complains to the farmer of her own weariness to get him to travel slowly.

2

परिचय

Gulliver (गुलिवर) Brobdingnag (ब्रॉबडिंगनाग) नामक स्थान पर था जहाँ के लोग तथा जानवर आकार में वृहद थे। उसे एक किसान ने पकड़ लिया जो उसे अपने घर ले गया तथा उसने और उसकी पत्नी ने उसके प्रति दयालुता का व्यवहार किया। प्रस्तुत पाठ में गुलिवर किसान की बेटी का वर्णन करता है, जिसने उसकी तब तक देखभाल की जब तक वह ब्रॉबडिंगनाग में रहा।

हम देखते हैं कि कैसे उसे Market (बाजार) ले जाया जाता था और फिर लोगों का Entertainment (मनोरंजन) करने के लिए मुख्य शहर ले जाया जाता था और कैसे किसान गुलिवर की थकान व दु:ख की चिंता किए बिना लगातार मंच प्रदर्शन करके धन कमाता था।

ग्लमडैलक्लिच किसान की पुत्री

Farmer (किसान) की पत्नी को 9 वर्ष की एक पुत्री थी, जो सिलाई में निपुण थी। उसने गुलिवर के लिए कुछ कपड़े सिले। उसने गुलिवर को ब्रॉबडिंगनाग की मातृभाषा भी सिखाई। उसने बच्चे के पालने को उसके बिस्तर की तरह तैयार किया। गुलिवर ने उसका नाम Glumdalclitch ('ग्लमडैलक्लिच') रखा।

गुलिवर का मंच पर कला प्रदर्शन

गुलिवर को एक Box (बक्से) में रखकर शहर के मुख्य बाजार में ले जाया गया। उसे Inn (सराय) के सबसे बड़े कमरे में रखी एक मेज पर रखा गया। ग्लमडैलक्लिच उसके नजदीक बैठ गई। एक साथ तीस व्यक्तियों से ज्यादा को उसे देखने की अनुमति नहीं थी।

किसान धन की अच्छी मात्रा प्राप्त करने लगा तथा वह उसे बार-बार बाजार तथा मुख्य शहर में ले जाने लगा। उसकी छोटी नर्स ग्लमडैलक्लिच सदैव उसके साथ रहती थी। उसे गुलिवर की थकान की परवाह थी और इसलिए उसने इस विषय में अपने पिता अर्थात् उस किसान को बताया।

Word Meaning

Dexterous	– कुशल	Contrived	– योजना बनाना
Preservation	– सुरक्षा	Requite	– कर्ज (दया का) चुकाना
Reverence	– आदर	Mirth	– खुशी, हर्ष
Vulgar	– असभ्य	Indignity	– अपमान
Ignominy	– तिरस्कार, अपयश	Reproach	– दोष लगाना, निंदनीय
Distress	– व्यथित, परेशान	Pursuant	– के अनुसार
Alighted	– जलता हुआ, नीचे आना	Diverting	– मनोरंजक
Fopperies	– मूर्खतापूर्ण प्रदर्शन	Vexation	– संताप, परेशानी
Sabbath	– विश्राम दिवस	Design	– योजना बनाना
Rivulet	– छोटी नदी	Pallisadoed	– ढका होना

Important Questions

Questions based on the Plot of the Chapter

Q 1. Explain in the detail the stage shows performed by Gulliver.

गुलिवर द्वारा किए जाने वाले स्टेज शो का विस्तार से वर्णन करें।

किसान का एक करीबी मित्र उससे मिलने आया – उसने किसान को सुझाव दिया कि वह बाजार में गुलिवर की प्रदर्शनी करे – अगले दिन, गुलिवर को पास के गाँव ले जाया गया – वे एक सराय में रुके – वहाँ किसान ने पूरे गाँव में समाचार पहुँचाने के लिए मुनादी वाले को रखा – तिनके के टुकड़े को भाले की भाँति चलाया – उस दिन उसे बारह समूह को प्रदर्शित किया गया – वह इतना थक गया था कि वहाँ से गिरने वाला था।

Ans. One day, a visitor to the farmer's family gave a suggestion to the farmer that, Gulliver should be taken on a market day of the next town and displayed to the people as an object of curiosity. The farmer could charge a small fee against the display. The farmer was very happy at this suggestion.

The next market day, the farmer took Gulliver and his daughter to the next village. They stopped at an inn. The farmer hired a town crier to spread the news. On the day of the show, Gulliver was placed on a large table in the largest room in the inn. His little nurse sat on a stool next to him to direct him in what he should do.

Thirty people were allowed at a time. Gulliver walked on the table. He answered the questions asked by Glumdalclitch. He bowed to the people, drank liquor from a thimble and drank to their health. He drew out his sword and flashed it in the air. Then the little nurse gave him a part of a straw which he exercised as a pike. He was shown to twelve sets of people till he was so tired that he was nearly dropping down where he stood.

Q 2. Had Gulliver had not laughed at the guest, he would not have had been taken to perform stage shows. How far is this statement true?

यदि गुलिवर ने उस मेहमान का मजाक नहीं उड़ाया होता, तो उसे स्टेज शो के लिए नहीं ले जाया जाता। यह कथन कहाँ तक सत्य है?

गुलिवर के आरामदायक जीवन का अंत उस दिन हो गया – किसान का एक मित्र गुलिवर को देखने आया – किसान ने गुलिवर को मेज पर खड़ा करके विभिन्न संक्रियाएँ करने को कहा – वह मेहमान अत्यंत वृद्ध था – उसने गुलिवर को देखने के लिए चश्मा पहना – चश्मे से उसकी आँखों को दो चंद्रमा समझकर गुलिवर हँस पड़ा – मेहमान ने इसे अपना अपमान समझा – बदला लेने के लिए उसने किसान को सुझाव दिया कि वह गुलिवर की प्रदर्शनी लगाए – अतः गुलिवर की मुसीबत उसकी खुद की बुलाई हुई थी – यदि वह उस मेहमान का अपमान नहीं करता – शायद वह इतने कठिन व थकावट वाले कार्य से बच जाता।

Ans. In Brobdingnag, Gulliver had a very comfortable life. The entire family took good care of him. But his comfortable and protected life lasted very soon, when one of the farmer's friend came to see him. When he came, the farmer put Gulliver on the table and made him takeout his sword and flash it and bow to the farmer and ask him "How do you do?" in his own language.

The visitor was an old man and could not see well, put on his spectacles to see Gulliver better. The sight of his eyes looking like two moons made Gulliver laugh, at which the rest of the family also laughed. The visitor was very angry at being laughed and soon took his revenge on Gulliver.

He suggested to the farmer that he should show Gulliver to the public on market days in the villages. That was the end of Gulliver's comfortable life as the farmer made Gulliver work very hard to stage his shows. Hence, his misery was self-invited. If he had not insulted the visitor, he would have not been put to such a difficult and tidious job.

Gulliver's Freedom from the Farmer's Clutches

As long as Gulliver stayed with the farmer, he had to perform stage shows many times a day. Instead of treating Gulliver as a human being, the farmer decided to make as much money as he could make through Gulliver before he happened to die. Meanwhile, the farmer receives a court order to bring Gulliver to the Queen for her entertainment. The Queen is delighted to see Gulliver and buys him for one thousand gold coins. Gulliver was reluctant to depart without his little nurse and pleaded to the Queen to take Glumdalclitch along with him so that she might be appointed his nurse once again.

Gulliver Presented to the Emperor

The Queen presented Gulliver to the emperor and asked him to repeat the tale of his woes. The emperor mistook Gulliver for a mechanical toy or a doll. Besides, Gulliver's story sounded incredible and baseless. They concluded that Gulliver was a freak of nature. Gulliver, unable to take it anymore, informed them that he belonged to a country inhabited by millions of people like him and of his size. The emperor gradually began to believe Gulliver's narrative. The emperor asked the Queen to keep inspecting Gulliver, which she did pleasurably as she had become a great fan of his.

Word Meaning

Insatiable – कभी संतुष्ट न होना
Demeanour – व्यवहार, आचरण
Impaired – कमजोर
Recompensed – दोबारा पैसा चुकाना
August – उच्च व सम्मानीय
The Creation – सुंदरता वाला व्यक्ति
Tether – वहाँ
Vassal – दास
Rabble – क्रुद्ध भीड़
Drudgery – नीरस काम
Inappropricties – अनुचित व्यवहार
Defectiveness – कमियाँ, त्रुटियाँ

3

गुलिवर की किसान के शिकंजे से मुक्ति

Gulliver (गुलिवर) जब तक किसान के साथ रहा तब तक उसे दिन में कई-कई बार अपनी कला दिखानी पड़ी। गुलिवर के साथ एक मानव की तरह व्यवहार करने के स्थान पर किसान ने गुलिवर की मृत्यु से पहले उसके द्वारा ज्यादा-से-ज्यादा धन कमाने का निश्चय किया। इस बीच में किसान को Queen (रानी) के पास उसका मनोरंजन करने के लिए गुलिवर को जाने का अदालत का आदेश मिलता है। रानी गुलिवर को देखकर खुश होती है और उसे Gold (सोने) के एक हजार सिक्कों में खरीद लेती है। परंतु गुलिवर अपनी छोटी नर्स के बिना जाने को तैयार नहीं था और उसने रानी से Glumadalclitch (ग्लमडैलक्लिच) को भी साथ लेने की विनती की जिससे वह एक बार फिर उसकी नर्स बन सके।

गुलिवर को सम्राट के समक्ष प्रस्तुत किया गया

रानी ने गुलिवर को Emperor (सम्राट) के समक्ष प्रस्तुत किया तथा उससे अपने दु:खों की कहानी दोहराने को कहा। सम्राट ने गुलिवर को एक Mechanial Toy (यांत्रिक खिलौना) या Doll (गुड़िया) समझा। इसके अतिरिक्त गुलिवर की कहानी भी मिथ्या एवं आधारहीन लगी। उन्होंने निष्कर्ष निकाला कि गुलिवर Nature (प्रकृति) द्वारा रची गई एक असामान्य रचना है। गुलिवर ने उन्हें बताया कि वह एक ऐसे देश का निवासी था जहाँ उसके जैसे और उसी के आकार के करोड़ों लोग निवास करते थे। सम्राट को धीरे-धीरे गुलिवर की कहानी पर विश्वास होने लगा। सम्राट ने रानी को गुलिवर पर नजर रखने के लिए कहा तथा जो उसने प्रसन्नतापूर्वक किया, क्योंकि वह स्वयं उसकी मुरीद हो गई थी।

Gravity	– गंभीर	Austere	– सख्त और संयमी
Dominions	– डराना	Contrived	– बनाना
Ingenious	– चालाक, कुशल	Concerted	– सुनियोजित
Rustic	– असभ्य, अशिष्ट	Quadrupeds	– चार पैरों वाला
Evince	– प्रदर्शित करना	Virtuosic	– विद्वान्
Lusus Nature	– प्रकृति की विषमता	Disdaining	– घृणास्पद
Occult	– रहस्यमयी	Piety	– निष्ठा

Important Questions

Questions based on the Plot of the Chapter

Q 1. Do you agree that the Queen's arrival was a disguised rebirth for Gulliver? Justify your answer.

आप इस बात से सहमत हैं कि रानी का आगमन गुलिवर का बदला हुआ पुनर्जन्म है तर्क सहित उत्तर दें।

लालच के कारण किसान गुलिवर के प्रदर्शन से अधिक से अधिक पैसा कमाना चाहता था – इससे गुलिवर के स्वास्थ्य पर प्रतिकूल प्रभाव पड़ा – वह कंकाल की भाँति हो गया – किसान समझ गया कि गुलिवर अब ज्यादा दिन तक जिंदा नहीं रह पाएगा – वह उससे और अधिक काम लेने लगा – तभी रानी के आगमन से गुलिवर के प्राणों की रक्षा हो गई – रानी ने गुलिवर को किसान से खरीद लिया – राजमहल में आकर गुलिवर का स्वास्थ्य सुधरने लगा – वह उसका पुनर्जन्म था – किसान के पास तो उसकी मृत्यु सुनिश्चित थी – रानी के पास आकर गुलिवर को दोबारा जीवन मिला।

Ans. The farmer was very greedy. He made maximum money out of Gulliver's shows by over exerting him. This overwork started showing its effect on Gulliver's health. It was quite obvious that Gulliver would not live for long. He was reduced to a skeleton. The farmer decided to exhibit him as much as he could before Gulliver finally died.

So, things got worse and worse till the Queen came in his life as a saviour. She was so overwhelmed with the show of Gulliver that she decided to buy him from the master. The master was thrilled as he didn't expect Gulliver to live for more than a month. He gladly sold him to the Queen. In the palace, Gulliver's spirits started reviving. It was his rebirth.

The Queen had given him a new life by purchasing him from his cruel master who had made him do such horrible work that he had nearly killed Gulliver in his plan to make money for himself. But the care and love of the Queen gave a new life to him and he survived.

Q 2. How did the Queen treat Gulliver throughout?

रानी गुलिवर के साथ किस प्रकार का व्यवहार करती थी?

ब्रॉबडिंगनाग की रानी गुलिवर को एकदम ही पसंद करने लगी – उसने किसान से उसे एक हजार सोने के सिक्कों के बदले खरीद लिया – उसने ग्लमडैलक्लिच को भी महल में रखा – गुलिवर के लिए एक अलग कक्ष बनवाया – कक्ष के चारों ओर गद्दे लगवाए जिससे गुलिवर को चोट न लगे – उस कक्ष में मेज व कुर्सियाँ रखवाई – गुलिवर की सभी सुख-सुविधाओं का ध्यान रखा – उसने गुलिवर के लिए आधुनिक वस्त्र सिलवाए – गुलिवर रानी के साथ चाँदी के बर्तनों में खाना खाता था – उसे गुलिवर का साथ पसंद था – बौने द्वारा गुलिवर को परेशान करने पर बौने को कोड़े लगवाए – उसने गुलिवर के जीवन को प्यार व खुशी से भर दिया था।

Ans. The Queen of Brobdingnag developed an instant liking for Gulliver. She purchased him from the farmer for a thousand pieces of gold. She was happy to grant Gulliver's wish to have Glumdalclitch stay at the palace. She was warm and kind hearted.

She got a comfortable bed chamber made for him from her own cabinet maker. This chamber was quilted on all sides to prevent any accident and also furnished with a couple of Chairs and tables.

She made sure that he was provided with every possible comfort and luxury. She got fashionable garments stitched for him Gulliver dined with the Queen in silver dishes and plates.

She took pleasure in his company. When her dwarf scared Gulliver played pranks to hurt, the Queen was furious and ordered him to be whipped. She displayed an affection for Gulliver and brought happiness into his life.

Introduction

Gulliver describes the country of Brobdingnag, the royal palace, kitchen and army and the chief temple. According to him, modern mapmakers in Europe committed a blunder in displaying only the sea between Japan and California. He proposes to correct modern maps by showing land between North-West parts of America and great continent of Tartary. He tells the readers how he used to travel in a particular box contrived for his convenience.

The Kingdom of Brobdingnag

The kingdom of Brobdingnag was a peninsula. It was six thousand miles in length and from three to five in breadth. The kingdom had fifty one cities and a number of villages. Lorbrulgrud, the capital of Brobdingnag, was the largest of the cities.

The Temple

Gulliver was very desirous to see the chief temple, especially the tower belonging to it. So, Gulliver and Glumdalclitch visit to see the temple, but Gulliver was disappointed as he expected it to be taller but which though beautiful, was not more than 3,000 feet in height.

The Royal Kitchen, Military and Stable

The royal kitchen was also wonderful. It was six hundred feet high. It had great pots and kettles, joints of meats on the spits. Gulliver was also mesmerised by the sight of the royal military guard on parade, in detachments of five hundred. The emperor had hundred of horses in his stable. They were, of course, enormous, 54 to 60 feet high. On state occasions, a militia guard of 500 horses used to accompany the emperor.

4

परिचय

Gulliver (गुलिवर) ने ब्रॉबडिंगनाग राज्य, Royal Palace (शाही महल), रसोईघर, Army (सेना) और मुख्य मंदिर का वर्णन किया। उसके अनुसार Europe (यूरोप) में आधुनिक मानचित्र निर्माताओं ने Japan (जापान) एवं California (कैलीफोर्निया) के मध्य मात्र समुद्र ही दिखाकर एक बड़ी भूल की है। उसने America (अमेरिका) के उत्तर-पश्चिमी भाग एवं Tartary (टार्टरी) द्वीप के मध्य जमीन दर्शाकर आधुनिक मानचित्रों को ठीक करने का सुझाव दिया। उसने पाठकों को यह बताया कि किस प्रकार वह एक विशेष बक्से में यात्रा किया करता था, जोकि उसके लिए उपयोगी एवं सुविधाजनक था।

ब्रॉबडिंगनाग साम्राज्य

Brobdingnag (ब्रॉबडिंगनाग) साम्राज्य Peninsula (प्रायद्वीपीय) संरचना वाला था। यह लंबाई में छ: सौ मील तथा चौड़ाई में, तीन सौ से पाँच सौ मील तक था। साम्राज्य में इक्यावन शहर एवं अनेक गाँव थे। ब्रॉबडिंगनाग राज्य की राजधानी Lorbrulgrud (लॉरब्रलग्रड) थी जो राज्य के शहरों में सबसे बड़ा था।

मंदिर

गुलिवर Chief Temple (मुख्य मंदिर) को देखने हेतु बहुत इच्छुक था, विशेष रूप से इस पर लगे टावर को। अत: गुलिवर एवं Glumdalclitch (ग्लमडैलक्लिच) मंदिर का भ्रमण करने गए परंतु गुलिवर को थोड़ी निराशा हुई, क्योंकि उसे उम्मीद थी कि मंदिर अधिक ऊँचा होगा परंतु वह सुंदर था, मंदिर 3,000 फीट से ज्यादा ऊँचा नहीं था।

शाही रसोईघर, सेना तथा घुड़साल

Royal Kitchen (शाही रसोईघर) भी अत्यंत शानदार था। इसकी ऊँचाई छ: सौ फीट थी। इसमें बड़े-बड़े बर्तन तथा केतलियाँ और सीकचे पर टंगा हुआ मांस था। गुलिवर Royal Military (शाही सैनिक) योद्धाओं की परेड को देखकर भी अचंभित रह गया जो पाँच सौ सैनिकों का एक विभाग था। सम्राट की Stable (घुड़साल) में लगभग सौ से अधिक की संख्या में घोड़े थे। नि:संदेह वे आकार में विशाल थे जिनकी ऊँचाई 54 से 60 फीट थी। विशिष्ट अवसरों पर सैनिकों का योद्धा समूह का नेतृत्वकर्ता लगभग 500 घोड़ों के साथ सम्राट के साथ चला करता था।

Word Meaning

Counterpoise	– संभव न होना	Impossible	– पार करना या निकलना
Terminated	– समाप्त करना	Manifest	– स्पष्ट
Edifice	– भव्य आकर्षक इमारत	Wen	– सूजन (एक प्रकार का ट्यूमर)
Reckoned	– अनुमान लगाना		
Rooted	– खोदना	Latticed	– ढकना

Important Questions

Questions based on the Plot of the Chapter

Q 1. Why does Gulliver ask the modern mapmakers in Europe to correct the maps?

गुलिवर आधुनिक नक्शा बनाने को यूरोप का नक्शा सही करने के लिए क्यों कहता है?

गुलिवर ब्रॉबडिंगनाग में आरामदायक जीवन बिता रहा था – वह राज्य का एक छोटा-सा वर्णन देता है – लॉरब्रुलग्रड छः हजार मील लंबा तथा तीन से पाँच हजार मील चौड़ा है – उसे लगता है कि भूगोलशास्त्री कितने गलत हैं – जब वे कहते हैं कि जापान तथा कैलिफोर्निया के मध्य केवल समुद्र है – गुलिवर को लगता है कि इन दोनों द्वीपों के मध्य भूमि होनी चाहिए, क्योंकि इतना विशाल समुद्र होना संभव नहीं है – टार्टरी के महाद्वीप को बराबर करने के लिए धरती का समानुपात होना आवश्यक है – अतः नक्शा बनाने वालों को अपने नक्शे व चार्ट को धरती के इस विशाल टुकड़े को अमेरिका के उत्तर पश्चिमी भाग से जोड़कर, ठीक कर लेना चाहिए।

Ans. Gulliver enjoyed his stay in this country of giants. He gave a short description of the Kingdom as he saw it, which was not much because he travelled with the Queen only who did not go further than two thousand miles out of the capital, Lorbrulgrud. The whole kingdom was about six thousand miles in length and three to five thousand miles in breadth. This only goes to show how wrong the geographers are when they say that there is nothing but sea between Japan and California. In fact, Gulliver felt that there had to be some land between these two continents, as it is not possible to have such a great sea. There must be a balance of earth to counterbalance the great continent of Tartary, therefore the mapmakers have to correct their maps and charts by joining this vast tract of land to the North-West part of America. This is the kingdom of Brobdingnag.

Q 2. Describe the royal army, the kitchen and the royal stable.

शाही सेना, रसोईघर तथा शाही अस्तबल का वर्णन करें।

शाही महल देखते हुए गुलिवर शाही रसोईघर में पहुँचता है – रसोईघर में चूल्हा दस कदम चौड़ा था – उसमें विशालकाय बर्तन, केतली इत्यादि रखे थे, राजा का अस्तबल भी शानदार था – इसमें छः सौ से अधिक घोड़े थे – ये घोड़े भी चौवन से साठ फीट ऊँचे थे – राज्य समारोहों के समय सम्राट के साथ पाँच सौ घोड़े चलते थे – सम्राट की सेना छोटी किंतु अनुशासित थी।

Ans. While visiting the palace of the emperor, Gulliver came across the kitchen. The emperor's kitchen was indeed a noble building, which was about six hundred feet high. The great oven was about ten paces wide. It had enormous sized kitchen grate, prodigious pots and kettles, joints of meats on the spits.

The emperor's stable was also very amazing. The emperor had above six hundred horses in his stable. Those horses were generally from fifty-four to sixty feet high. On state occasions, a military guard of five hundred horse accompany the king. So, the king didn't have a large army but despite its limited size, it was very disciplined.

Q 3. Why was Gulliver disappointed to see the chief temple of the city?

गुलिवर मुख्य मंदिर को देखकर निराश क्यों हुआ?

गुलिवर वहाँ का मुख्य मंदिर देखने के लिए बहुत उत्सुक था – ग्लमडैलक्लिच उसे वहाँ लेकर गई – गुलिवर मंदिर को देखकर निराश हुआ, क्योंकि मंदिर की ऊँचाई तीन हजार फीट थी – जोकि ब्रॉबडिंगनाग के लोगों के लिए अधिक नहीं थी – मंदिर अत्यंत सुंदर व मजबूत था – उसकी दीवारें सौ फीट मोटी थीं।

Ans. Gulliver was very keen to seen the chief temple and the tower belonging to it, as it was supposed to be the highest in the kingdom. And so, one day, his little nurse carried him there, but he was very disappointed to see it because the height of the temple was not above three thousand feet, which was not too high for the people of Brobdingnag. But it was beautifully made and was strong. The walls, which were a hundred feet thick, were made of rough stones and decorated with statues of Gods and Goddesses cut in marble. Those statues were larger than life statues and were placed in their several corners. Hence, Gulliver was not much happy to see the chief temple, but he was impressed with its beauty and grandure.

Accidents

Gulliver's life in Brobdingnag was very smooth and comfortable, but his diminutive size always exposed him to various hard accidents. He is safe neither in palace nor outside. The Queen's dwarf always tried to amuse himself by playing practical jokes on Gulliver. Once, he was whipped but in vain. One day when Glumdalclitch was carrying Gulliver into the royal garden, the dwarf quietly followed them.

One day Glumdalclitch left Gulliver in the palace garden and got preoccupied talking to her governess. The gardener returned Gulliver to Glumdalclitch, though she severely scolded Gulliver. Gulliver witnessed an execution of a criminal in Brobdingnag. The criminal was fixed in a chair upon an erected platform and his head cut off in one blow with a sword of about forty feet long. His body produced a fountain of blood. The spectacle was really unbearable.

दुर्घटनाएँ

Gulliver (गुलिवर) का जीवन Brobdingnag (ब्रॉबडिंगनाग) राज्य में अत्यंत शांत और सहजपूर्वक था, परंतु छोटे आकार के कारण उसे विभिन्न प्रकार की गंभीर समस्याओं का भी सामना करना पड़ता था। वह ना तो महल में ही सुरक्षित था एवं ना ही महल के बाहर। रानी का Dwarf (बौना) सेवक सदैव गुलिवर के साथ मज़ाक करके अपना मन बहलाने की कोशिश करता था। एक बार उसे चाबुक से मारा भी गया, परंतु यह व्यर्थ रहा। एक दिन जब Glumdalclitch (ग्लमडैलक्लिच) गुलिवर को लेकर Royal Garden (शाही बगीचे) में जा रही थीं तब उस बौने व्यक्ति ने चुपचाप उनका पीछा किया।

एक दिन ग्लमडैलक्लिच ने गुलिवर को शाही बगीचे में अकेला छोड़ दिया तथा स्वयं स्वामिनी से बातें करने लगी। बगीचे के स्वामी ने गुलिवर को वापस ग्लमडैलक्लिच को लौटाया तब उसने चेतावनी भरे लहजे में गुलिवर को डाँटा। गुलिवर ने ब्रॉबडिंगनाग राज्य में एक अपराधी को मृत्युदंड दिए जाने का दृश्य भी देखा। उस अपराधी को एक कुर्सी पर बैठाकर बाँध दिया गया तथा चालीस फीट लंबी Sword (तलवार) से उसका गला काट दिया गया। उसके शरीर से Blood (रक्त) की धार फूट पड़ी। यह दृश्य वास्तव में असहनीय था।

Word Meaning

Allusion	– तुलना करना	Malicious	– दुर्भावना
Rogue	– शरारती, नटखट, आवारा	Provocation	– क्रोध का कारण
Entreated	– याचना करना	Agonies	– दर्द
Severely	– सख्ती से	Reprimanded	– डाँटना
Resolutely	– दृढ़तापूर्वक	Espalier	– पौधा

Important Questions

Question based on the Plot of the Chapter

Q 1. Describe the several accidents Gulliver met with and their impact on him.

गुलिवर के साथ हुई प्रत्येक दुर्घटना का तथा इस पर उनके प्रभाव का वर्णन कीजिए।

ब्रॉबडिंगनाग में रहते हुए गुलिवर को अनेक दुर्घटनाओं का सामना करना पड़ा – बौने ने उसके सिर के ऊपर सेब का पेड़ हिला दिया – बड़े आकार के सेबों से गुलिवर बुरी तरह घायल हो गया – ओलों की बारिश से गुलिवर के शरीर पर अनेक चोट के निशान थे – एक बार नौका चलाते समय सेविका ने गुलिवर को गलती से नहर में गिरा दिया।

Ans. Gulliver faced a lot of mishaps during his stay at Brobdingnag. The dwarf seized a chance to take revenge on him by shaking an apple tree right over his head as Gulliver was walking under it. The poor man was hit on the back by one of these gignatic fruits and he fell down flat on his face. At another occasion, Gulliver was caught in a hailstorm. A more dangerous incident occurred when he was alone in the garden and the gardener's small white spaniel picked him up in his mouth and ran to his master. Luckily, this well-trained dog carried him safely without hurting him. Glumdalclitch got very angry and severely scolded the gardener.

A linnet, whom he was able to hit, gave him tough time. Once while rowing, the governess almost dropped him in the trough of water. Another time, one of the servant's carelessness let a huge frog into the trough. Gulliver banged it with his scull and forced it to leap out. The funniest incident, however, was when a monkey pulled Gulliver out of his box, took him to the roof and fed him some food forcibly. This incident made Gulliver sick for almost ten days.

Gulliver Made the Comb, the Chairs and the Purse

Once or twice a week, Gulliver attended the emperor levee, a kind of reception held every morning when the emperor got out of bed. Gulliver often saw him under the barber's hand. Gulliver asked the barber to give him some of the lather foams, out of which he picked forty or fifty of the strongest stumps of hair. Then, he made a comb with a piece of fine wood, fixing the stumps of hair on the wood.

Gulliver Played the Spinet

The emperor was fond of music. So, he frequently held music competitions and invited Gulliver. But due to loudness of music, Gulliver failed to enjoy it. As everything was prodigious in size, so was music, louder than all the drums and trumpets in the British army. With the help of two heavy sticks, Gulliver ran up and down a long table, beating the spinet with sticks and playing tunes for the royal couple. Gulliver had learnt in his youth to play the piano, so he decided to divert the emperor and the Queen.

The Emperor's Conclusion

English history just sounded like a heap of murders, massacres and revolutions to the emperor. Gulliver failed to convince the emperor of the greatness of England, as the emperor called England a pack of corrupt, unqualified, greedy dacoits. He further believed that most Englishmen must be a disgusting, evil bunch of little creeps.

6

गुलिवर ने कंघी, कुर्सियाँ एवं पर्स बनाने का कार्य किया

Gulliver (गुलिवर) सप्ताह में एक या दो बार Emperor (सम्राट) द्वारा आयोजित की जाने वाली Levee (राज्यसभा) में शामिल होता था, जो प्रत्येक सुबह सम्राट के उठने के पश्चात् आयोजित की जाने वाली सभा थी। गुलिवर ने उसे अनेक बार Barber (नाई) के पास ही देखा था। गुलिवर ने नाई से उसे बचा हुआ Lather Foams (झाग) देने को कहा, जिसमें से उसने चालीस-पचास मजबूत बाल चुने। फिर उसने उत्तम कोटि की लकड़ी का प्रयोग करके बालों को लकड़ी में गाड़कर एक Comb (कंघा) बनाया।

गुलिवर ने स्पिनेट बजाया

सम्राट को संगीत में अत्यंत रुचि थी। अत: वह अपने साम्राज्य में संगीत प्रतिस्पर्द्धाओं का आयोजन कराता है और गुलिवर को भी आमंत्रित करता था, परंतु संगीत की ध्वनि अत्यधिक तेज होने के कारण गुलिवर इसका आनंद नहीं ले पाया, क्योंकि प्रत्येक वस्तु आकार में अत्यंत वृहद थी। अत: संगीत के स्वर British Army (ब्रिटिश सेना) के Drums (ड्रमों) तथा Trumpets (ट्रमपेटों) से भी ऊँचे थे। दो भारी छड़ों की मदद से गुलिवर एक लंबी मेज के ऊपर व नीचे दौड़ने लगा, छड़ों से स्पिनेट बजाया तथा शाही जोड़े के लिए संगीत बजाने लगा। गुलिवर ने अपनी युवावस्था में पियानो बजाना सीखा था। अत: उसने सम्राट व रानी का मनोरंजन करने का निश्चय किया।

सम्राट का निष्कर्ष

England (इंग्लैंड) का इतिहास सम्राट के Murders, Massacres and Revolutions (हत्याओं, नरसंहारों एवं क्रांतियों) का भंडार प्रतीत हुआ। गुलिवर सम्राट को इंग्लैंड की अच्छाई में नाकाम रहा, क्योंकि सम्राट ने इंग्लैंड को भ्रष्ट, लुटेरे एवं अयोग्य लोगों का समूह करार दे दिया। साथ ही उसने यह भी मान लिया कि अधिकतर अंग्रेज घृणास्पद, रेंगने वाले कीड़ों की प्रजाति थे।

Word Meaning

Scourge	– अभिशाप, कड़ा दण्ड देना	Contemptuously	– तिरस्कारपूर्वक
Strutting	– सावधानीपूर्वक चलना	Prating	– बंदरों की चिल्लाहट
Dwindled	– क्षीण या कम हो जाना	Mortified	– लज्जाजनक
Verily	– ईमानदारी से	Insolent	– असम्मानजनक
Swagger	– शेखी मारना	Malicious	– दुष्ट
Nettled	– झुंझलाहट	Scurvy	– नीच
Vexed	– उत्तेजित	Cashiered	– बर्खास्त करना
Repartees	– बुद्धिमानीपूर्ण वार्तालाप	Entreaty	– प्रार्थना करना
Intercede	– दूसरे के लिए याचना करना	Odious	– घृणास्पद
Rallied	– मजाक करना	Victuals	– भोजन देने वाला
Excrement	– अपशिष्ट	Spawn	– बच्चे
Dexterity	– कुशल	Confounding	– भ्रमित करने वाला
Dispatched	– मार डालना		

Important Questions

Q 1. What three articles did Gulliver make and present to the emperor, Queen and his little nurse?

गुलिवर ने किन तीन वस्तुओं को बनाकर सम्राट रानी तथा छोटी नर्स को भेंट किया।

गुलिवर हफ्ते में एक या दो बार सम्राट से मिलने जाता था। उसने सम्राट के नाई से झाग देने की विनती की। उसमें से चालीस – पचास बाल चुनकर उसने अपने लिए कंघी बनाई। रानी की नौकरानी से रानी के बाल लेकर दो कुर्सियाँ बनाई। उन्हें उसने रानी को भेंट किया। उसने इन बालों से एक छोटा-सा पर्स बनाया। इसे ग्लमडैलक्लिच को भेंट किया। इसमें ग्लमडैक्लिच ने अपनी छोटी चीजों को रखा।

Ans. Gulliver visited the Emperor once or twice a week, while the Emperor was having his tea or getting a shave by his barber. One day, Gulliver asked the barber to keep some of the lather. He washed it and separated some of the tough strands of the Emperor's hair.

He took a piece of very thick wood and pierced holes in it and fixed the hair in each hole and made a nice comb. In the same way, he asked the Queen's maid to some of the Queen's hair. He got the frames of the chairs ready from the carpenter. He wove the hair through the small holes, he made in the frames.

These chairs, he presented to the Queen who was delighted with the present. Of the rest of the hair, he made a small purse for Glumdalclitch which she could not use, as it was weak to hold any coins. So, she would only store small knick-knacks in it.

Q 2. Gulliver tried to play the piano and divert the Emperor and the Queen but in vain. Why?

गुलिवर ने पियानो बजाकर सम्राट तथा रानी का मनोरंजन करना चाहा लेकिन असफल रहा। क्यों?

सम्राट को संगीत का बहुत शौक था। महल में अक्सर संगीत के कार्यक्रम आयोजित किए जाने थे। गुलिवर भी स्पिनेट (एक छोटा पियानो) बजाकर सम्राट व रानी का मनोरंजन करना चाहता था, लेकिन स्पिनेट साठ फीट बड़ा था। प्रत्येक कुंजी एक फुट चौड़ी थी। गुलिवर का हाथ उन पर नहीं पहुँच सकता था। उन्हें दबाने के लिए अधिक जोर लगाना पड़ता था। उसने दो डंडों के सिरों को चूहे की खाल से ढक दिया। स्पिनेट के सामने चार फीट नीचे एक बेंच रखी गई। स्पिनेट बजाने के लिए गुलिवर को इस बेंच पर दौड़कर डंडों की सहायता से कुंजी को दबाना पड़ता था। एक धुन बजाने में उसे लगभग एक मील दौड़ना पड़ा। वह शाही जोड़े का मनोरंजन नहीं कर सकता और अत्यंत थक गया।

Ans. The emperor was very fond of listening to music and would often take Gulliver to some concert held in the palace. He could also play the spinet (a small piano), which he had learned in his youth. One day, he thought to entertain the Emperor and Queen with an English tune upon this instrument. But this was extremely difficult because the spinet was nearly sixty feet long and each key was almost a foot wide.

Gulliver could not reach to above five keys and to press them down required a hard stroke with his fist. So, he planned a method. He prepared two round sticks, which were thicker at one end than the other. He covered the thicker end with the pieces of a mouse's skin. A bench was placed before the spinet that was about four feet below the keys.

For playing the spinet, Gulliver would run sliding upon it, that way and this, as fast as he could, banging the proper keys with his two sticks and playing tunes for the emperor and the Queen. In this exercise, Gulliver had to run a mile to play the whole tune. He could not divert the royal couple and got extremely tired by this unusual exercise.

The Emperor's Stupidity and Ignorance Established

In the previous chapter, the emperor criticised England intensely. He called English history, a pile of murders, massacres and revolutions. Reacting silently, Gulliver convinces us that we should pardon the Brobdingnagian emperor for his intense criticism of England. Actually, the emperor did not know better because his own country was cut off from all the other nations of the world.

Gulliver wants to inform us about ignorance and stupidity of the emperor. Gulliver proposed to the emperor to display the formula to make gunpowder to subdue his adversaries and to strengthen his militia.

Well-Disciplined Army

The army was well-disciplined since all of its soldiers are farmers and tradesmen who serve under their own landlords and chief citizens without pay or reward. The infantry comprised one hundred and seventy-six thousand foot. The cavalry contained thirty two thousand horse. The Emperor bothers to have armies though there are no other countries nearby.

Word Meaning

Word	Meaning	Word	Meaning
Resentment	– अप्रसन्नता	Concealing	– छिपाना
Ridicule	– मजाक बनाना	Inquisitive	– उत्सुकता
Vivdication	– न्याय स्थापना, समर्थन	Eluded	– हाथ न आना
Laudable	– सराहनीय	Partiality	– पक्षपात
Frailties	– कमजोरियाँ	Beauties	– सुंदरता
Endeavour	– प्रयत्न करना	Discourses	– बातचीत
Prejudices	– पूर्वाग्रह	Exconpted	– छूट-प्राप्त
Conrfined	– सीमित	Imgratiate	– अनुग्रह प्राप्त करना

सम्राट की मूर्खता एवं अज्ञानता प्रमाणित हो गई

पूर्व अध्याय में Emperor (सम्राट) ने उत्तेजना से England (इंग्लैंड) की आलोचना की। उसने इंग्लैंड के इतिहास को हत्या, नरसंहार एवं क्रांतियों का भंडार करार दिया। शांतिपूर्वक व्यवहार करते हुए Gulliver (गुलिवर) हमें यह निश्चय कराता है कि हमें Brobdingnag (ब्रॉबडिंगनाग) के सम्राट को उसके इंग्लैंड के बारे में कटु वक्तव्यों के लिए क्षमा कर देना चाहिए। वास्तव में, सम्राट अनभिज्ञ था, क्योंकि उसका साम्राज्य विश्व के अन्य भागों से पूर्णतया पृथक् था। गुलिवर हमें सम्राट की मूर्खता तथा अज्ञानता के विषय में बताना चाहता है।

गुलिवर सम्राट को Gunpowder (बारूद) बनाने की विधि बताने का प्रस्ताव देता है, जिससे सम्राट अपने दुश्मनों को नेस्तनाबूत कर सके तथा अपनी सेना को मजबूत बना सके।

अनुशासित सेना

सेना भली-भाँति अनुशासित थी, क्योंकि इसके सभी सिपाही Farmer (किसान) या व्यवसायी थे जो बिना वेतन या इनाम के अपने स्वामी या मुख्य नागरिकों हेतु कार्य करते थे। Infantry (पैदल सेना) में एक सौ छिहत्तर हजार सैनिक थे। घुड़सवारी सेना में बत्तीस हजार घोड़े थे। सम्राट सेना को लेकर चिंतित रहा करता था, यद्यपि आस-पास कोई देश नहीं था।

Kindle	– जाग्रत करना	Agitation	– आंदोलन, उत्तेजना
Rammed	– भरना	Batter	– मारना, कूटना
Masts	– पाल	Rigging	– जहाज की रस्सी
Besieging	– घेराबंदी	Rip	– फटना
Dashing	– जोरदार	Imgredients	– घटक
Resoponding	– जमा करना	Importent	– शक्तिहीन, कमजोर
Gravelling	– महत्त्वहीन	Desolation	– सूनापन
Contriver	– निर्माता, बनाने वाला	Privy	– जानकारी से संबंधित
Veveration	– आदर		

Important Questions

Questions based on the Plot of the Chapter

Q 1. Describe the method of making gunpowder narrated by to the Brobdingnagian emperor.

गुलिवर द्वारा ब्रॉबडिंगनाग के सम्राट को बताई गई बारूद बनाने की विधि का वर्णन करें।

गुलिवर सम्राट के प्रति अपनी कृतज्ञता प्रकट करने के लिए उसे बारूद बनाने की विधि बताने का सुझाव देता है – वह बताता है कि यह पाउडर खोखली नली में भर कर लौहे के गोले को तेजी से फेंकने का काम करता है – जिससे भयानक रूप से विनाश होता है – इस बारूद को लोहे के गोले में भर कर इंजन (तोप) की सहायता से किसी भी शहर पर गिराया जा सकता है – जिससे वृहत रूप से पूरा शहर तबाह हो सकता है – वह सम्राट को इसकी विधि उसके कारीगरों को सिखाने का प्रस्ताव देता है – वह बताता है कि इसके लिए प्रयुक्त सामग्री सस्ती व आसानी से मिल जाती है – किंतु गुलिवर की आशा के विपरीत सम्राट इसमें उत्सुकता नहीं दिखाता है – वह इस अमानवीय प्रस्ताव को सुनकर भयभीत हो जाता है – इस प्रस्ताव को ठुकरा देता है।

Ans. Gulliver wanted to express his gratitude for all the royal favours given to him by the emperor. So, he told the emperor that he know about the ingredients and the method of making a powder that is a sure instrument of destruction. A proper quantity of this powder is filled into a hollow tube of brass or iron.

It would drive a ball of iron as lead with such a speed that nothing could often stop its farce. These largest ball would destroy a whole city causing wide spread death and destruction.

This powder is often put into larger hollow balls of iron and discharged them by an engine (canon) into some city. This causes massive destruction. Gulliver further told the emperor that ingredients of his powder were very cheap and common.

He knew the way of mixing them and could instruct his workmen how to make it. Contrary to his expectations rather than showing his eagerness and interest in the offer, the emperor was horrified to hear such an inhuman proposal. He declined the offer.

Q 2. The Emperor criticised England without any authorisation. He asked Gulliver never to mention the gunpowder if he valued his life. The Emperor called Gulliver an insect, impotent and grovelling. Write a character sketch of the Emperor in light of the statement.

सम्राट ने बिना किसी अधिकार के इंग्लैंड की आलोचना की। उसने गुलिवर से बारूद की चर्चा करने से मना किया यदि वह अपनी जान बचाना चाहता था। सम्राट ने गुलिवर को कीड़ा, तथा नपुंसक कहा। इस कथन के प्रकाश में सम्राट के चरित्र का चित्रण करें।

गुलिवर सम्राट का सम्मान पाने के लिए उसे बारूद बनाना सिखाने का प्रस्ताव दिया है – बारूद के विनाशकारी परिणाम को जानकर सम्राट भयभीत हो गया – इससे पता चलता है कि वह एक विवेकी संवेदनशील व नैतिक मूल्यों को मानने वाला था – वह दयालु तथा उदार व्यक्ति जिसके लिए नैतिक मूल्य सर्वोपरि थे – वह एक सरल व शांतिप्रिय व्यक्ति था जोकि सत्ता या लालच के लिए पागल नहीं था – उसके लिए सत्ता का अर्थ सामान्य ज्ञान, विवेकशीलता तथा न्याय था – अतः उसने बारूद बनाने की कला को सीखने से मना कर दिया – वह एक संवेदनशीला व्यक्ति था जो दिखावे को नापसंद करता था तथा एक व्यावहारिक दृष्टिकोण रखता था।

Ans. Gulliver knew that the emperor had formed unfavourable opinion about English life. The emperor was isolated from the rest of the world. He could not comprehend about the situations in Europian countries. So, Gulliver once tried to gain favour by offering to teach him the method of making gunpowder, which was unknown in Brobdingnag, after describing its lethal effects in warfare.

The emperor was horrified at such an inhuman idea. It showed that the emperor was a wise, sensible and morally upright man. He was kind and generous and attached great importance to morality. He was also a gentle and peace loving man who was not obsessed with power or greed. For him, governing meant commonsense, reason, justice and leniency.

Therefore, he was not ready to learn the art of manufacturing a destructive agent just to overawe his subjects. Thus, he was a very sensible person who disliked to show off and had a very practical approach.

8

Gulliver's Box Snagged by an Eagle

One day the emperor and the Queen, accompanied by Gulliver and Glumdalclitch, went on a tour of the South coast of the kingdom. The emperor stayed in his palace near Flanflasnic, an English city eighteen miles away from the sea coast. Gulliver asked the servant to take him to the beach, instructing Glumdalclitch to stay in the palace. The servant carried Gulliver's travelling box down to the beach.

The servant left Gulliver's box on the beach and went among the rocks to look for the birds' eggs. Suddenly, Gulliver felt a sudden jolt and woke up. The box happened to be snagged by an eagle. Gulliver felt swimming in the air at a speed. The eagle flew high and then dropped Gulliver's box. Gulliver was worried about Glumdalclitch as she was surely going to be blamed by the Queen for his loss.

Gulliver Fell into the Sea

He was safe from the eagle but he was scared lest he should die floating, starved and feeling cold. He heard some sort of grating noise on that side of the box where the staples were fixed. Gulliver felt by the bobbing of his box that he was at sea. Gulliver called out in all the languages he knew. Then he tied his handkerchief to a stick he usually carried. Thrusting the stick up the hole, Gulliver waved it repeatedly in the air. A sailor saw a hole in the side of his box and Gulliver emerged very tired and weak.

Gulliver's Narrative—Imaginary and Incredible

The sailors salvaged some of the contents of Gulliver's box. The captain of the ship, Thomas Wilcox, inquired Gulliver about his whereabouts. Gulliver narrated the entire tale, but the captain thought that Gulliver was crazy or a convict sent to sea in a giant box as punishment.

8

गुलिवर के बक्से को चील द्वारा ले जाया जाना

एक दिन सम्राट एवं रानी Gulliver (गुलिवर) एवं Glumdalclitch (ग्लमडैलक्लिच) के साथ साम्राज्य के दक्षिणी तट पर भ्रमण हेतु गए। Flanflasnic (फ्लैनफ्लैस्निक) के निकट अपने महल में ही ठहर गया, जोकि समुद्र तट से अठ्ठारह मील की दूरी पर शहर था। गुलिवर ने इस वजह से ग्लमडैलक्लिच को महल में ही विश्राम करने की सलाह दी तथा नौकर से स्वयं को समुद्र तट पर ले चलने को कहा। नौकर गुलिवर के यात्रा हेतु निर्मित बक्से को लेकर समुद्र तट की ओर चल पड़ा।

नौकर ने गुलिवर के बक्से को समुद्र तट पर छोड़ दिया तथा स्वयं चिड़िया के अंडो की तलाश करने के लिए पहाड़ों के बीच चला गया। अचानक गुलिवर को झटका लगा एवं वह उठ गया। उस बक्से को एक Eagle (चील) ने उठा लिया था। गुलिवर को लगा जैसे वह हवा में तीव्र गति से तैर रहा हो। चील ऊँचाई पर उड़ने लगी तथा उसने गुलिवर के बक्से को छोड़ दिया। गुलिवर को ग्लमडैलक्लिच की चिंता हो रही थी, क्योंकि उसके खोने का कसूर रानी अवश्य उसी पर मढ़ देने वाली थी।

गुलिवर समुद्र में गिर गया

वह चील से बच गया, परंतु उसे चिंता सता रही थी कि कहीं ठंड से Starve (भूख) से तथा तैरते हुए उसकी मृत्यु ना हो जाए। अचानक उसने बक्से की कुंडी वाली दिशा में कुछ हलचल होने की आवाज सुनी। बक्से के तैरने के कारण गुलिवर को अनुभव हो गया कि वह समुद्र में है। गुलिवर सभी भाषाओं में, जिन्हें वह जानता था, चिल्लाया। इसके पश्चात् उसने अपने रुमाल को जिसे वह हमेशा अपने साथ रखता था, एक छड़ी से बाँध दिया। Stick (छड़ी) को छेद से बाहर निकालकर गुलिवर लगातार उसे हवा में हिलाता रहा। एक नाविक ने बक्से के किनारे पर छेद देखा, जिसमें से उसे थका हुआ एवं दुर्बल गुलिवर नजर आया।

गुलिवर का व्याख्यान-काल्पनिक एवं अविश्वसनीय

Sailors (नाविकों) ने गुलिवर के बक्से से कुछ सामान को नष्ट होने से बचा लिया। जहाज के कप्तान Thomas Wilcox (थॉमस विलकॉक्स) ने गुलिवर से पूछा कि वह कहाँ से आया है। गुलिवर ने उसे सारी कहानी बता दी, परंतु कप्तान को लगा कि गुलिवर पागल है या वो कोई कैदी है जिसे सजा के तौर पर बक्से में बंद करके समुद्र में छोड़ दिया गया है।

Word Meaning

Impulse	– तीव्र	Conjecture	– अनुमान लगाना
Tumbiel	– हाथ से खींचने वाली गाड़ी	Propagate	– फैलाना
Deliverance	– आजादी	Groove	– नाली जैसा
Fatigued	– थकान	Page	– नौकर
Foreboding	– पूर्वाभास, अपशकुनी	Sashes	– दुपट्टा
Wistful	– विचारपूर्ण	Clefts	– दरार
Devour	– खाना, निगलना	Quarry	– शिकार
Buffets	– हवा के थपेड़े	Cataract	– महाजल प्रपात, बड़ा झरना
Stifled	– दम घोटने जैसा	Crannies	– दरार/छेद
Endeavouced	– प्रयास	Disconsolate	– दुखी, अप्रसन्न
Grating	– सख्त, कड़ा		

Important Questions

Questions based on the Plot of the Chapter

Q 1. Describe how Gulliver's travelling box was snagged and dropped into the sea by an eagle.

गुलिवर के बक्से को कैसे चील द्वारा झपटा मारकर उठाया तथा समुद्र में फेंका गया, इसका वर्णन करे।

गुलिवर ने ब्रॉबडिंगनाग में दो वर्ष बिता लिए थे – तीसरे वर्ष के आरंभ में वह ग्लमडैलक्लिच, सम्राट तथा रानी से अठ्ठारह मील दूर एक महल में रुके – गुलिवर समुद्र देखने के लिए बेचैन हो रहा था – ग्लमडैलक्लिच को महल में छोड़कर वह एक नौकर के साथ समुद्र तट पर आ गया – गुलिवर डर से चीखने अचानक वह तेजी से नीचे गिरने लगा – गुलिवर ने देखा कि वह समुद्र में गिर गया – गुलिवर अब इतने बड़े समुद्र में अहसहाय व अकेला था।

Ans. Gulliver had spent two years in Brobdingnag. About the beginning of the third year, Glumdalclitch and he accompanied the emperor and Queen on a tour to the South coast of the kingdom. Gulliver was carried in his travelling box. When they came to their journey's end, the Emperor decided to stay for a few days at a palace, eighteen Eurpeon miles away from the sea.

Gulliver longed to see the ocean but Glumdalclitch had a bad cold, so a servant took him to the seaside. The servant set his box on some rocks.

Gulliver lifted his curtains and looked out to sea. He then decided to have a nap on his hammock and shut the curtain and lay down. He was suddenly woken up by a hard tug upon the ring which was fixed on the top of the box. He felt the box rise high up in the air and then being moved at a fast speed. He shouted out several times but there was no answer. He looked out of the window and saw only sky and clouds. An eagle had taken the ring in his beak and was going to fly off somewhere. Gulliver could hear the fettering of wings. Suddenly, he felt himself falling at a great speed. His falls was stopped by a terrible splash. He had fallen into the sea. Gulliver was alone in a wide sea, trapped in a box helpless and lonely.

Q 2. Describe how Gulliver was traced and rescued by the sailors.

गुलिवर को कैसे नाविकों द्वारा पीछा किया तथा बचाया गया, वर्णन करें।

चील ने गुलिवर के बक्से को समुद्र में गिरा दिया – गुलिवर को भूख व ठंड के कारण मर जाने का भय सताने लगा – अचानक उसे बाहर कुछ आवजें सुनाई दीं – उसे लगा कि उसके बक्से को समुद्र की सतह में खींचा जा रहा है – वह हर भाषा में जोर-जोर से चिल्लाने लगा – उसने एक छड़ी के साथ अपना रुमाल बाह्य कर छेद से बाहर निकाला और तेजी से रुमाल हिलाने लगा – एक जहाज के कप्तान ने सबसे पहले उस बक्से को बहते देखा – पास आने पर उसने देखा कि वह कोई जहाज न होकर एक बड़ा बक्सा था – उसने गुलिवर की छड़ी व रुमाल को भी देख लिया – उसने अनुमान लगाया कि इसमें कोई वद्किस्मत इंसान बंद है – उसने अपने आदमियों से कहकर बक्से को खींचवा लिया – नाविकों ने बक्से को काटकर गुलिवर को बाहर निकाला।

Ans. When the box of Gulliver was dropped by the eagle in the sea, Gulliver got horrified. He was sure to die of starvation and cold in the next few days. Suddenly, he heard some noise outside. Soon he felt as if the box was being pulled along the sea surface. This gave him some hope that he might be getting rescued. He shouted in all the languages. Then he tied a handkerchief to a stick and waved it out of the hole. It was the captain of the ship who first of all spotted Gulliver's box in the sea.

The captain mistook it for a sail of another vessel. However, on coming near, he discovered his error. So, he sent his long boat to investigate further. On detecting a stick with Gulliver's handkerchief, he concluded that there must be some unfortunate man inside. So, the captain got his men to tow this 'chest' to ship. The sailors sawed a hole in the box and Gulliver was pulled out.

QUESTION DIGEST

Term I

Questions Based on the Plot of the Chapter

Q 1. Describe the amazing spectacle that Gulliver beheld in the form of flying island.

गुलिवर के हतप्रभ कर देने वाले दृश्य का वर्णन करो जोकि फ्लाइंग आईसलैंड के रूप में सामने आया

Ans. After being set a drift on a canoe by the pirates, Gulliver went to many islands, which were all uninhabited and rocky. When he came to the last island, he was introduced to a wonderful phenomenon : flying island. While Gulliver was walking is the island, all of a sudden the shining sun became obscure and he observed a vast moving opaque object between himself and the sun. It was a firm body.

On minute observation, Gulliver saw people inside it. Gulliver was astonished beyond description to see an island in the air and the people of the island controlling its motions and movements. Its sides were encompassed with several gradations of galleries and stairs at fixed intervals to descend from one to the other. When Gulliver approached the people, they also made signs to him and lowered a chain to pull him on to the floating island.

Q 2. Give an account as to how the king of Laputa submitted the territories below on the continet to obedience, if they refused to obey him.

लपुता के राजा ने दुश्मनों को नीचा दिखाने के लिए उनकी आज्ञा को अस्वीकार क्यों किया।

Ans. The king of Laputa administered and controlled the territories below on the continent by the sheer advantage offered by the floating island. If any town disobeyed the king, engaged in rebellion or mutiny or refused to pay the tribute, the king restroed to two methods to reduce them to obedience.

it would result in disease and deprivation. If the magnitude of the crime was greater, they could also be pelted with big stones from above so that they had no defence except taking refuge in their cellars or cave, while the roofs of their house would be crumbled. In case the subjects offered further resistance, the king could resort to the last extreme remedy of dropping the island directly upon the heads of the people; thereby causing the total destruction of men and property. But the king seldom took to this extreme step.

Q 3. Describe the event that took place forty years ago in Lagado. What were its repercussions?

लगादो में चालीस साल पहले घटना का वर्णन करे। इसके नतीजे क्या हुए।

Ans. About forty years ago, some people of Lagado went to Laputa, they acquired a little knowledge of mathematics. On coming back, they sought to change the management of all arts, sciences, languages, mechanics upon a new order. With the royal consent, they established an academy of projectors in Lagado and eventually many such academies were established in almost every town of the kingdom. These academies gave new rules and methods for the management of everything : agriculture, manufactures, construction etc.

The fall out of this new system, which had not reached perfection, was that the entire country lay waste, the house were in ruin, the people were without food and clothes. It was indeed a very bleak and hopeless scenario. Those who followed the previous system were looked down upon as selfish people and enemies of innovation, who preferred their personal comforts to the general improvement of the country.

Q 4. Describe the cause of Gulliver's disappointment.

गुलिवर की निराशा का विस्तार से वर्णन कीजिए।

Ans. Gulliver desired to see the personalities of modern history : of the royal families with their ancestors of eight to nine generations. But to his utter dismay, he found that the purity of the royal blood was not intact. Infact, it had been corrupted by the people of base instincts. Gulliver felt disgusted at the thought that modern history was distorted by the mean writers, who twisted the facts and misled the world. They attributed rewards to the most undeserving of people and condemned the virtuous.

The history credited cowards, traitors, flatterers and did grave injustice to the brave, honest, innocent and excellent people. Gulliver saw many instances where virture was made to suffer ignominy and vice was honoured. He found that the corruption and degeneration of humanity had reached its utmost height in the society.

All this had a very saddening effect on Gulliver and he longed to see some yeoman, who symbolished the virtues of by gone era.

Q 5. Gulliver, at first, felt elated at the description of Struldbrugs, but afterwards his delight turned into sadness. Explain.

गुलिवर ने पहली यात्रा स्ट्रलडबर्स के विवरण पर उत्तेजित महसूस किया, परन्तु बाद में उसकी खुशी उदासी में बदल गयी विवरण करे।

Ans. In Luggnagg, Gulliver came to know of a special kind of people called Struldbrugs, who were immortals. Their births were very rare and only a matter of chance. They were distinguished by a spot on the forehead. Gulliver was filled with delight on hearing the account of such people.

He, at length, expressed his own desires of what he would do if he were born a Struldbrug. But he was soon acquainted with the reality, which was far from being amusing. He realised that the perpetual life did not mean perpetuity of youth, health and vitality. The Struldbrugs, he was told, also succumbed to the effects of old age. With the passage of time, they lost memory, health, hair, teeth and apetite. At that stage, they could not even converse with others because they could not keep pace with the changing language of the country.

They could not enjoy life like the young people nor die like the mortals, but were condemned to a perpetual existence. On hearing all this, Gulliver lost the desire of an eternal life, even the prospect of a cruel death appeared better to Gulliver than a never ending life.

Question based on the Character-Sketch

Q 6. How was Lord Munodi different from the other people of Lagado?

लार्ड मुनौदी लगादो के लोगों से कैसे अलग था।

Ans. Lord Munodi was a person of rank. He was the Governor of Lagado. He was man of common sense and prudence and understood the wrong approach of his countrymen in applying the system of a particular nation on Lagado.

He was also very well aware of the visionless plans of his countrymen, who despised him for not following their example. His country house and lands were the only impressive features in an otherwise barren and unimpressive Lagado. He was admired by Gulliver, who observed that he was 'free from those defects, which folly and beggary had produced in others'. He was kind and hospitable and welcomed Gulliver his house.

Q 7. Give your opinion about the emperor of Luggnagg in the light of his dealings with Gulliver.

सम्राट का लगनेज के विषय मे गुलिवर के साथ समझौते के बारे मे वर्णन कीजिए।

Ans. The persona of the emperor is revealed by the strict laws and rules concerning court etiquettes: paying obscience to the king, rules regarding strangers and hospitality to guests. The emperor appeared as an absolute monarch, strict and just ruler. His hospitable nature is apparent from the way he treated Gulliver by providing him a lodging in the court and a daily allowance for maintenance and gold for common expenses.

He was an admirer of virtue and desired Gulliver to stay in the court and accept some employment in the court. He was also generous and understanding, he graciously granted licence to Gulliver to leave when the latter refused his offer and desired to return his own country. He also recommended Gulliver to the king of Japan.

Part III **1** Term II

Introduction

Gulliver set out on his third voyage. Firstly, he along with his crew was hit by a storm. Then he was chased by pirates. Finally, the pirates set him free in a canoe with insufficient food. Gulliver had to manage with the bird's eggs. He arrived at a floating island named Laputa.

Gulliver Set Out on his Third Voyage

Gulliver's wife had forbidden him to set on any further voyage in future, when he seemed to go nuts having returned from Brobdingnag, but he could not overcome his love for sea and set out on his third voyage having stayed at home just for ten days.

Gulliver was visited by his old friend Captain William Robinson, who offered him a position on his ship, as a surgeon.

Hit by the Storm and Chased by the Pirates

They arrived at Fort St George. Having stayed there for three weeks, they arrived at Fort Tonquin. The captain had to stay alone in Tonquin for several months, but he wanted to do business there. He bought a canoe and appointed Gulliver its master.

Within three days, their ship was hit by a storm and on the tenth day, they were attacked by some pirates who wanted Gulliver and his companions to be tied and thrown into the sea. They captivated Gulliver. Gulliver spoke Dutch and told who they were.

1

परिचय

Gulliver (गुलिवर) अपनी तृतीय समुद्र यात्रा पर रवाना होता है। सर्वप्रथम, उसे अपने सहयोगी दल के साथ तूफान का सामना करना पड़ा। इसके पश्चात् Pirates (समुद्री डाकुओं) ने उसका पीछा किया। अंततः समुद्री डाकू उसे एक छोटी नौका में अपर्याप्त भोजन के साथ छोड़ देते हैं। गुलिवर को चिड़िया के अंडों को भोजन के रूप में प्रयोग कर अपना गुजारा करना पड़ा। अंततः वह एक तैरते हुए द्वीप Laputa (लापुता) पर पहुँच जाता है।

गुलिवर की तृतीय समुद्री यात्रा

गुलिवर की पत्नी ने उसे भविष्य में किसी भी समुद्री यात्रा पर जाने से मना कर दिया था क्योंकि Brobdingnag (ब्रॉबडिंगनाग) से लौटने के बाद गुलिवर का व्यवहार विचित्र हो गया था, परंतु गुलिवर अपनी समुद्री यात्रा के मोह को छोड़ नहीं सका एवं मात्र 10 दिन घर पर रुकने के पश्चात् वह तृतीय समुद्री यात्रा पर चल पड़ा।

गुलिवर से उसके पुराने मित्र Captain William Robinson (कप्तान विलियम रॉबिन्सन) ने मुलाकात की तथा उसे अपने जहाज पर शल्य चिकित्सक के रूप में कार्य करने का निमंत्रण दिया।

तूफान का प्रहार एवं समुद्री डाकुओं द्वारा पीछा

वे St George (सेंट जॉर्ज) Fort (किला) पहुँच गए। वहाँ तीन सप्ताह तक रुकने के पश्चात् वे Tonquin (टॉनक्विन) किला पहुँच गए। कप्तान को टॉनक्विन में काफी महीनों तक अकेले रहना पड़ा, किंतु वह वहाँ व्यापार करना चाहता था। उसने एक छोटी नौका खरीदी तथा गुलिवर को उस नौका का मालिक नियुक्त किया।

तीन दिन के अंदर ही उनके जहाज पर तूफान का हमला हो गया तथा दसवें दिन उन पर समुद्री डाकुओं ने हमला कर दिया, जोकि गुलिवर एवं उसके साथियों को बाँधकर समुद्र में फेंक देना चाहते थे। उन्होंने गुलिवर को बंधक बना लिया। गुलिवर उनसे Dutch (डच) भाषा में बात करने लगा तथा उसने उन्हें बताया कि वे कौन थे।

Gulliver was Set Free in a Separate Canoe

The pirate's captain finally divided Gulliver's crew between their two ships and set Gulliver free in a small canoe with provisions just for four days. He saw many islands on his way. He went to each and every island one by one. They were all desolate and rocky. He saved his provisions and tried to survive with bird's eggs. He roasted the eggs on an open fire and passed his night in the shelter of rocks. Thus, Gulliver used his canoe to row to some tiny local islands nearby, but he could find neither much food nor shelter in any of them.

गुलिवर को अलग नौका में रिहा कर दिया गया

डाकुओं के Captain (कप्तान) ने अंततः गुलिवर के दल को दो जहाजों के मध्य बाँट दिया तथा छोटी नौका में मात्र चार दिनों के सामान के साथ गुलिवर को मुक्त कर दिया। उसने रास्ते में अनेक द्वीप देखे। वह बारी-बारी से प्रत्येक द्वीप पर गया। वे सारे द्वीप निर्जन एवं पहाड़ी से भरे हुए थे। उसने अपने सामान का भंडार बचाए रखा तथा चिड़िया के अंडों को भोजन के रूप में प्रयोग करके ज्यादा समय तक जीवित रहने की कोशिश की। वह अंडों को खुले आसमान के नीचे पकाता था। तथा पहाड़ों की शरण में रातें बिताता था। अतः गुलिवर अपनी नौका के सहारे किसी नजदीक के छोटे द्वीप की तलाश करने लगा, परंतु उसे कहीं भी पर्याप्त मात्रा में भोजन या शरण नहीं मिल पाई।

Laputa—The Floating Island

While standing on the fifth and last island, Gulliver saw a shadow blot out the sun. He took out his telescope, looked up and saw that it was an island in the air, inhabited by people. This was the island of Laputa. Gulliver managed to signal to these people for help and they finally looked down and let down a chain for Gulliver to climb up. They pulled Gulliver on to the floating island.

लापुता-तैरता हुआ द्वीप

पाँचवें एवं अंतिम द्वीप पर खड़े होकर गुलिवर ने एक छाया देखी जो सूर्य को ढक रही थी। उसने अपनी दूरबीन निकाली, ऊपर देखा और पाया कि वह हवा में तैरता हुआ एक द्वीप था, जिस पर लोग रह रहे थे। यह लापुता द्वीप था। गुलिवर ने मदद हेतु उन लोगों की ओर संकेत किया और अंततः उन्होंने नीचे देखा एवं एक जंजीर लटका दी, जिससे गुलिवर ऊपर चढ़ सके। उन्होंने गुलिवर को तैरते हुए द्वीप पर खींच लिया।

Word Meaning

Cornish	– क्रोनवाल स्थान से संबंधित	Stout	– बड़ा और भारी
Apprehend	– आशंका करना	Engagement	– सहमति
Defray	– भुगतान करना	Sloop	– एक छोटी कश्ती
Pinioned	– बँधा हुआ	Pirates	– समुद्री डाकू
Countenance	– चेहरे की भाव भंगिमा	Jabbering	– जल्दी-जल्दी बोलना
Canoe	– खेने वाली छोटी नौका	Strewing	– फैलाना
Heath	– छोटा, कठोर सदाबहार पौधा	Parched	– सूखा हुआ
Desolate	– अकेला	Desponding	– निराशा
Listless	– बिना किसी ऊर्जा	Obscure	– धुंधला
Circumpectly	– सावधानीपूर्वक	Interposition	– गतिरोध
Conjecture	– अनुमान लगाना	Distress	– चिंतित, चिंतातुर
Traffic	– लेन-देन के व्यापार में लिप्त		

Important Questions

Questions based on the Plot of the Chapter

Q 1. Describe the hardships Gulliver faced before arriving at the floating island.

तैरते हुए द्वीप पर पहुँचने से पूर्व गुलिवर को किन कठिनाइयों का सामना करना पड़ा? वर्णन कीजिए।

शुरू में तीसरी यात्रा आरामदायक होना – टॉनक्विन पर कप्तान ने व्यापार करने का निश्चय किया – उसने एक छोटी नौका में सामान भरकर गुलिवर व चौदह नाविकों को आस-पास के द्वीपों पर उन्हें बेचने के लिए भेजा – तीसरे दिन समुद्री तूफान का शिकार हो गए – दसवें दिन समुद्री डाकुओं ने उनका पीछा किया – डाकुओं ने उन सभी को बाँध दिया – उनकी नौका की तलाशी ली, बाद में चौदह नाविकों को एक जहाज पर भेज दिया – गुलिवर को एक कश्ती में चार दिन की भोजन सामग्री देकर समुद्र में छोड़ दिया – चार दिन तक गुलिवर एक द्वीप से दूसरे द्वीप तक पक्षियों के अंडे खाकर घूमता रहा – आखिरी द्वीप पर उसे हवा में तैरती एक वस्तु दिखी – वह तैरता द्वीप लापुता था।

Ans. Initially, the third voyage went on smoothly till Gulliver and his reached fort Tonquin. The captain decided to stay there for some time. Then he bought a sloop. He loaded the sloop with some merchandise and sent fourteen men under the charge of Gulliver to trade the goods in the neighbouring islands.

In about three days' time, they were faced with a storm, which subsided after five days. On the tenth day, they were chased by two pirate ships. The pirates tied Gulliver and his companions. They searched the sloop.

A Dutchman among the pirates wanted them all to be killed. However, the two pirates took pity on them. The fouteen men were sent to the two ships, but Gulliver was set adrift in a small canoe with paddles and a sail. It had provisions only for four days. He was left to die in the sea. For four days, Gulliver sailed from island to island living on the birds' eggs that he collected from here and there. When he reached the last island in sight, he was very worried.

As he walked on this island in the scorching heat of the sun, he suddenly spotted a huge opaque body between himself and the sun. It was Laputa island, the floating island.

Q 2. Describe his encounter with the pirates and the final outcome.

गुलिवर द्वारा समुद्री डाकुओं का सामना करने तथा उसके परिणाम का वर्णन कीजिए।

गुलिवर अपने चौदह नाविकों के साथ सामान बेचने के लिए एक छोटे जहाज में निकला – उनका जहाज समुद्री तूफान में घिर गया – दसवें दिन समुद्री डाकुओं के दो जहाजों ने उनका पीछा किया – डाकुओं ने उन सभी नाविकों व गुलिवर को बाँध दिया – उन डाकुओं में से एक डाकू डच था, गुलिवर ने डच भाषा में उससे उन सबको छोड़ने की विनती की और कहा कि वे पड़ोसी देश के नागरिक हैं और ईसाई हैं – इस पर डच व्यक्ति अधिक नाराज हो गया – उसने गुलिवर से बदला लेने के लिए चौदह नाविकों को बाँटकर अलग-अलग जहाजों में भेज दिया – गुलिवर को अकेले एक कश्ती में बैठाकर समुद्र में छोड़ दिया – जापानी डाकू ने गुलिवर की कश्ती में चार दिन की भोजन सामग्री रखवा दी – एक घंटे तक गुलिवर कई द्वीपों पर घूमता रहा।

Ans. When Gulliver and his fourteen men set sail in a small ship for selling the goods to the nearby islands, a strong storm blew them off. They were driven for five days to the North-East and then further East.

On the tenth day, they were overtaken by pirates and as their ship was heavy with supplies, they were not able to outrun the pirates. The pirates had two ships. They tied Gulliver and his men up and their ship was searched.

One of the pirates was a Dutchman. So, Gulliver pleaded in Dutch language and asked them to leave him and his men as they were of neighbouring countries and both were Christians. The Dutchman got more angry on being called Christian. He took his revenge on Gulliver in an awful way. He provided the fourteen men, half for one ship and half for the other. Gulliver was to be set upon a canoe and let adrift. He was filled with horror and fear at the thought of having to fend for himself in the dangerous waters, but he had no choice. However, the kind Japanese captain had put some food into his canoe, enough to last him for four days. About an hour, he wandered on several islands to the South-East.

Q 3. How did Gulliver pass his days when he was set free in a canoe with the provisions just for four days?

गुलिवर ने अपने वे दिन कैसे बिताए जब उसे छोटी कश्ती में चार दिन की भोजन सामग्री के साथ छोड़ दिया गया था?

गुलिवर के जहाज पर डाकुओं ने कब्जा कर लिया – वे गुलिवर व उसके साथियों को बाँधकर समुद्र में फेंकना चाहते थे – गुलिवर द्वारा विनती करने पर उसे उसके साथियों से अलग करके एक छोटी नौका में थोड़ी-सी भोजन सामग्री देकर समुद्र में छोड़ दिया – थोड़ी दूर जाने पर गुलिवर को कई द्वीप दिखाई दिए – पहले द्वीप पर वह थोड़ी देर में ही पहुँच गया – वह द्वीप सुनसान था तथा भूमि अनुपजाऊ और पथरीली थी – उसे पक्षियों के घोंसले मिले – गुलिवर ने आग में पक्षियों के अंडे भूनकर खाए – दूसरे दिन से अन्य द्वीपों पर पहुँचा – सभी द्वीप सुनसान तथा अनुपजाऊ थे – गुलिवर को अपनी मृत्यु का डर सताने लगा – आखिरी दिन में एक गुफा में रहकर उसने रात बिताई।

Ans. When the boat of Gulliver was captured by the pirates, they wanted to throw Gulliver and his men in the sea. Gulliver pleaded for mercy and at last he was separated from his companions. They made Gulliver sail in a canoe with little food. When Gulliver sailed little farther, he found himself in sight of several islands to the South-East.

He reached the island in hardly any time. The first island was not inhabited and the land was barren and rocky. He found some birds' nests and made a fire and cooked the eggs from the nests. He spent the first night on that island and the next day set sail for the other ones. All were uninhabited and the land was infertile. Gulliver was feeling sorry for himself and was sure that he would die on those islands. He passed the night in a sad state in a cave which he found on the last island.

Strange People

Gulliver finds it strange about such people in Laputa. They all look quite odd with their heads tilted to one side or the other. One eye is turned inward and the other looks up. Their clothes have images of heavenly bodies. Some of them are servants. Each of them carries a 'flapper'. It is made of a stick with a pouch tied to the end. Their job is to assist the conversation between the listener and the speaker.

Gulliver is taken to the emperor. He sits behind a table full of mathematical instruments. The emperor is aroused from his thoughts after about an hour or so with the help of a 'flapper'. The emperor says something and Gulliver's ear is struck with the flapper. Gulliver tells that he doesn't need such an aid to listen to the emperor. Both Gulliver and the emperor do not understand each other because of their languages. So Gulliver is sent to his apartment thereafter.

Fond of Mathematics and Music

Soon a teacher is appointed to teach Gulliver the language of the island. Very soon he is able to learn the language. He discovers that the name of the island is 'Laputa'. 'Laputa' in their language means 'floating island'. A tailor is sent to Gulliver to make clothes for him. Meanwhile the emperor orders that the island is removed. It is taken to a point above the capital city of the kingdom Lagado. While moving it receives petitions from the subjects about various things. These are collected with the help of ropes sent down to the villages below.

The Laputans value mathematical and musical concepts too much. They also value theoretical disciplines above everything. They hate practical geometry and take care that their houses have no right angles. They are very good with charts and figures but are not so in practical matters. They practise astrology and dread changes in the heavenly bodies.

2

विचित्र लोग

Laputa (लापुता) में ऐसे व्यक्तियों के बारे में Gulliver (गुलिवर) यह आश्चर्यचकित मानता है। वे सभी सिरों के एक तरफ या दूसरी तरफ झुके हुए होने के कारण काफी अजीब दिखते हैं। एक आँख अंदर की तरफ मुड़ी और दूसरी ऊपर देखती है। उनके कपड़ों पर स्वर्गीय वस्तुओं के प्रतिबिंब हैं। उनमें से कुछ नौकर हैं। उनमें से प्रत्येक के पास एक 'flapper' (फ्लैपर) है। यह एक डंडे का बना है, जिसके एक सिरे में एक जेब बँधी है। उनका कार्य सुनने वाले और कहने वाले के बीच बातचीत में सहायता करना हैं।

गुलिवर को सम्राट के पास ले जाया जाता है। वह गणित के यंत्रों से भरी एक मेज के पीछे बैठता है। एक Flapper (फ्लैपर) की सहायता से लगभग एक घंटे के पश्चात् सम्राट को अपने विचारों से उठाया जाता है। सम्राट कुछ कहता है और गुलिवर के कान पर फ्लैपर के साथ हल्के से मारा जाता है। गुलिवर बताता है कि उसे सम्राट के साथ बातचीत करने के लिए ऐसी किसी चीज की आवश्यकता नहीं है। अपनी भाषाओं के कारण गुलिवर और सम्राट कुछ समझ नहीं पाते, इसलिए गुलिवर को उसके बाद उसके Apartment (अपार्टमेंट) में भेज दिया जाता है।

गणित तथा संगीत प्रिय लोग

शीघ्र ही गुलिवर को द्वीप की भाषा पढ़ाने के लिए एक अध्यापक की नियुक्ति की जाती है। बहुत शीघ्र वह भाषा को सीखने के योग्य हो जाता है। वह पाता है कि द्वीप का नाम लापुता है। उसकी भाषा में लापुता का अर्थ है Floating Island ('तैरता द्वीप')। गुलिवर के पास एक दर्जी उसके लिए कपड़े बनाने के लिए भेज दिया जाता है। इस बीच सम्राट आदेश देता है कि द्वीप को हटाया जाए। यह राजधानी शहर Lagado (लगाडो) के ऊपर एक बिंदु पर ले जाया जाता है। चलते हुए इसे कई चीजों के बारे में जनता से प्रार्थना-पत्र मिलते हैं। इन्हें नीचे गाँवों तक रस्से लटकाकर उनकी सहायता से इकट्ठा किया जाता है।

लापुतावासी गणित और संगीत के सिद्धांतों को काफी मानते हैं। वह Theory (विधियों) को प्रत्येक चीज से अधिक मानते हैं। उन्हें प्रयोगात्मक Geometry (ज्यामितीय) से काफी घृणा है और वे ध्यान रखते हैं कि उनके घरों में कोई दायाँ कोण न हो। वे चार्ट और आकृतियों में बहुत निपुण हैं, परंतु प्रयोगात्मक चीजों में इतने अच्छे नहीं हैं। वे ज्योतिष विद्या का प्रयोग करते हैं और स्वर्गीय चीजों में बदलाव से डरते हैं।

Word Meaning

Alighting	– धरती पर उतरना	Singular	– विशेष प्रकार का
Reclined	– झुका हुआ	Adorned	– सजाना
Flail	– हत्थे वाला लंबा हथियार	Speculations	– विवेचना करना
Discourses	– बातचीत, वार्तालाप	Taction	– स्पर्श करने की कला
Diligently	– सावधानीपूर्वक	Cogitation	– गहरे विचारों में डूबना
Manifest	– प्रदर्शित करना	Precipice	– पर्वत की ढलान
Jostling	– धक्का देना	Kennel	– रास्ते के गटर
Disengaged	– बिना कार्य के	Concourse	– एकत्रित होना
Rhomboides	– चतुर्भुज के आकार की	Cycloid	– वृत्ताकार
Trussed up	– बँधा होना	Hautboys	– लकड़ी का बना वाद्ययंत्र
Zenith	– आसमान का सबसे ऊँचा बिंदु	Ueal	– बछड़े का मांस

Important Questions

Questions based on the Plot of the Chapter

Q 1. Describe the features and dresses of Laputians.

लापुतावासियों की विशेषताओं तथा वस्त्रों का वर्णन करें।

↗ उड़ते द्वीप पर गुलिवर को विचित्र लोगों ने घेर लिया – उनके सिर दाएँ या बाएँ मुड़े रहते थे – उनकी एक आँख अंदर की ओर मुड़ती थी और दूसरी सीधे आसमान की ओर – उनके वस्त्रों पर सितारों तथा चंद्रमा की विभिन्न आकृतियाँ बनी थीं – वाद्य यंत्रों के चित्र भी बने हुए थे – उन विचित्र प्राणियों का अपने नौकरों या सेवकों द्वारा जिन्हें 'मक्खीमार' कहा जाता था, अनुकरण किया जाता था – उनके स्वामी सदैव गहरे चिंतन और विचारों में डूबे रहते थे – उनके सेवकों द्वारा उनका ध्यान आकर्षित करने के लिए उन्हें फ्लैपरों द्वारा आँख या कान पर थपथपाया जाता था – इस प्रकार वे एक-दूसरे से वार्तालाप करते थे।

Ans. On the flying island, Gulliver was surrounded by many people. They looked at him with great surprise and wonder. These people had very strange shapes and sizes. All of them had head that were either leaning to the left or the right, some had eyes that always looked towards the sky, some had eyes that looked inwrds. The clothes were designed with stars and shapes of moon and sun and woven with designs of fiddles, harps, guitars and many other instruments of music unknown to Gulliver. Many of these people were followed by servants.

These servants carried in their hands a stick to which was attached a balloon shaped object. In each balloon, were some dried peas or small pebbles. With this object, the servants now and then hit their masters on the eyes or mouth. They had to draw the attention of their masters who were always lost in intense speculations.

They were so much lost that they could neither speak nor listen to others. And so, when two people are about to talk, the servant taps the mouth of the person who is about to speak and the right ear of the person who is spoken to. These servants are called 'flappers' and only those who can afford them keep one.

Q 2. Describe their love for mathematics and music.

उनके संगीत तथा गणित के प्रति लगाव का वर्णन करिए।

लापुतावासियों की गणित और संगीत में रुचि थी – वे दूसरी चीजों की तनिक भी परवाह नहीं करते थे – वे अपने विचारों को लाइनों और आकारों द्वारा प्रकट करते थे – भोजन की वस्तुएँ तथा बर्तन भी ज्यामितीय आकृति के थे – मीट को समबाहु त्रिकोण में काटा गया था – गाय के मांस को समानांतर षड्फलक में और पुडिंग को एक चक्राभ में काटा गया था – दूसरी वस्तुओं को वाद्य यंत्रों का आकार जैसे कि हार्प, फिडल और अलगोजे का आकार दिया गया था अपने विचारों को प्रकट करने के लिए वे गणित व विज्ञान के शब्दों का प्रयोग करते थे – वे प्रत्येक वस्तु की प्रशंसा ज्यामितीय आकृति से तुलना द्वारा करते थे – यहाँ तक कि स्त्रियों की सुंदरता का वर्णन भी वे वृत्तों तथा समानांतर चतुर्भुजों द्वारा करते थे – वे केवल संगीत तथा गणित में ही निपुण थे – उनकी तार्किक तथा चिंतन क्षमता बहुत ही खराब थी।

Ans. The people of the flying island had a deep interest in music and mathematics. Both these fields roused their speculations and interest and kept them occupied. Their ideas found expressions through lines and figures. All dishes were prepared in mathematical or musical instruments shape. The mutton was shaped as an equilateral triangle, a piece of beef cut into a rhomboid and a pudding into a cycloid.

Even sausages and puddings looked like flutes and oboes. The servants cut the bread into cones, cylinders and parallelograms and several other mathematical figures. They used the phraseology of these two sciences to express their ideas. They praised anything worthy by comparing it to geometrical shapes. Even to describe the beauty of a woman, they used circles and parallelograms or the musical terms. They were good at mathematics and music only. They had very poor reasoning and imagination.

Functioning of Laputa

Gulliver finds the island is exactly circular. It consists of 10,000 acres of land. There is a cave at the centre and it is meant for astronomers. It has many kinds of instruments. There is also a lodestone six yards long. It moves the island with its magnetic force. It has two charges that can be reversed by means of an attached control. The island is capable of moving over the country beneath it. When the emperor wants to punish a particular region of the country, he keeps the island above it. That way he deprives the region of sun and rain. These inhabitants had plans to kill the emperor. The plan was to make the island come so low as to trap it and have control over it to take over the government.

लापुता की कार्यप्रणाली

Gulliver (गुलिवर) द्वीप को बिल्कुल गोल पाता है। इसमें 10,000 एकड़ भूमि है। केंद्र में एक गुफा है और यह Astronomers (खगोलशास्त्रियों) के लिए है। इसमें कई प्रकार के यंत्र हैं। छः गज लंबा एक Lodestone भी है। यह चुंबकीय ताकत के साथ द्वीप को खींचता है। इसमें दो चार्ज हैं जिन्हें एक जुड़े हुए कंट्रोल द्वारा वापस किया जा सकता है। द्वीप इसके नीचे देश के ऊपर चलने के योग्य है। जब Emperor (सम्राट) देश के किसी खास इलाके को सजा देना चाहता है तो वह द्वीप को इसके ऊपर रखता है। इस प्रकार वह उस इलाके को Sun (सूर्य) और वर्षा से वंचित रखता है। इन वासियों की सम्राट को मारने की योजना थी। योजना द्वीप को इतना नीचे लाने की थी कि इसे पकड़ा जाए और सरकार हथियाने के लिए इस पर नियंत्रण किया जाए।

Word Meaning

Declivity	– ढलान	Rivulets	– छोटी नदी
Exhaled	– वाष्पित	Chasm	– एक गहरी दरार या छेद
Astrolabes	– दूरी नापने का यंत्र	Concave	– वक्रीय भाग
Endued	– उपलब्ध	Oblique	– तिरछा
Diffused	– विसरित	Evidently	– स्पष्ट रूप से

Important Questions

Questions based on the Plot of the Chapter

Q 1. Describe how Laputa functioned.

लापुता द्वीप कैसे घूमता था? वर्णन कीजिए।

लापुता द्वीप वृत्ताकार था – इतने विशालकाय पिंड का घूमना अत्यंत आश्चर्यजनक था – इसका कारण एक चुंबक था – जो छः फुट लंबा और तीन फुट चौड़ा था – इसी की सहायता से द्वीप को ऊपर-नीचे और इधर-उधर घुमाया जाता था – चुंबक का धनात्मक ध्रुव धरती की ओर होता था तब द्वीप नीचे हो जाता था – जब ऋणात्मक ध्रुव नीचे होता था तब यह ऊपर उठ जाता था – तिरछा होने पर यह विपरीत दिशा में चलता था – क्षितिज से समानांतर होने पर द्वीप स्थिर हो जाता था – अतः द्वीप को इसी चुंबक की सहायता से ऊपर, नीचे व स्थिर किया जाता था – किंतु द्वीप को सम्राट के धरती पर स्थित स्वामित्व क्षेत्र के बाहर नहीं ले जा सकते थे – इसे धरती से चार मील से अधिक ऊपर नहीं उठा सकते थे।

Ans. The flying island is circular with a diameter of about four miles and a half. It is really interesting to know how such a gigantic body managed to move. It is an enormous sized loadstone or magnet, which is 6 yards in length and three in thickness.

The entire fate of the island depends on this loadstone or magnet. The loadstone was held in that position by a very strong axle of adamant passing through its middle. This loadstone and axle are responsible for the movement of the island.

When the positive pole of the magnet points towards the earth, the island descends and when the negative pole points downwards, it ascends. When the position of the stone is oblique, the motion of the island takes a corresponding direction. When the stone is put parallel to the horizon, the island comes to a standstill.

Thus, the island can be made to move rise, fall and standstill at will. The loadstone had the limitations. It could not move beyond the extent of the emperor's dominions below on the earth. It couldn't rise up for more than 4 miles.

Gulliver Leaves Island

Gulliver finds that the Laputans are more interested in mathematics, music etc, rather than anything. He finds them more superior to him and feels neglected in such a place. He wants to leave this island as he is not interested in anything. He finds one lord of the court different from the inhabitants.

They look at him as stupid but Gulliver finds him intelligent. Also he doesn't care for the music. Gulliver asks him to petition the emperor on his behalf to let him leave the island for Balnibarbi. Gulliver is allowed to leave it and reaches Balnibarbi.

Gulliver Visits Lord Munodi

He visits another lord named Munodi, who invites him to stay at his home. Gulliver and Munodi visit a nearby town where Gulliver finds people living in dirty surroundings and poorly dressed. The condition of the people is miserable.

The land is badly cultivated. They go to Munodi's estate which is green and fertile. Munodi tells Gulliver that other lords criticize him heavily for the mismanagement of his land.

Munodi tells Gulliver what happened there forty years ago. Some people visited Laputa and came with new ideas about art and mathematics. They decided to set up an academy in Lagado to do research in agriculture. They would also focus to improve the lives of the inhabitants through various projects and schemes. But these things did not happen. Munodi asks Gulliver to visit this academy. Gulliver is glad to do so as he already had a desire to know more such things.

4

गुलिवर द्वीप छोड़ता है।

Gulliver (गुलिवर) पाता है कि Laputa (लापुता) वासी किसी और चीज की बजाय गणित, संगीत आदि में अधिक आनंद लेते हैं। वह उन्हें अपने आप से ज्यादा उत्तम मानता है और ऐसे स्थान में अपेक्षित महसूस करता है। वह इस द्वीप को छोड़ना चाहता है, क्योंकि वह किसी और चीज में दिलचस्पी नहीं लेता। वह अदालत के एक लॉर्ड को दूसरे वासियों से भिन्न पाता है।

वे उसे मूर्ख मानते हैं, परंतु गुलिवर उसे होशियार पाता है। वह संगीत की भी परवाह नहीं करता। गुलिवर उसे उसके Balnibarbi (बालनीबार्बी) द्वीप जाने के लिए उसकी तरफ से सम्राट को प्रार्थना-पत्र देने के लिए कहता है। गुलिवर को उसे छोड़ने की अनुमति मिल जाती है और वह बालनीबार्बी पहुँच जाता है।

गुलिवर लॉर्ड मुनोडी के पास जाता है।

वह दूसरे लॉर्ड Munodi (मुनोडी) के पास जाता है, जो उसे उसके घर रहने के लिए कहता है जहाँ गुलिवर और मुनोडी नजदीक के कस्बे में रहने जाते हैं। जहाँ गुलिवर आदमियों को गंदे स्थानों पर रहते हुए और कम कपड़े पहने हुए पाता है। आदमियों की हालत दयनीय है।

भूमि पर बुरी तरह की खेती होती है। वे मुनोडी के Estate (एस्टेट) जाते हैं, जो उपजाऊ और हरा-भरा है। मुनोडी गुलिवर को बताता है कि दूसरे लॉर्ड उसकी भूमि को ठीक न रखने के लिए उसकी अधिक आलोचना करते हैं।

मुनोडी गुलिवर को बताता है कि चालीस वर्ष पहले वहाँ क्या हुआ था। कुछ आदमियों ने लापुता की यात्रा की और कला व गणित में नए विचारें के साथ आए। खेती में नई खोज करने के लिए उन्होंने Lagado (लागाडो) में एक अकादमी स्थापित करने का निर्णय लिया। वे प्रोजेक्टों और योजनाओं द्वारा वासियों के जीवन को उन्नत करने के लिए ध्यान देने लगे।

Word Meaning

Weary	– थका होना	Esteem	– आदर-सम्मान
Unversed	– बिना ज्ञान के	Abstracted	– ख्यालों में खोए रहना
Rendered	– निर्मित, बनाया	Contemptible	– घृणास्पद
Used	– बर्ताव करना	Reckoned	– समझना
Eminent	– प्रसिद्ध	Detractors	– दूसरों को बदनाम करने वाले
Illustrious	– प्रसिद्ध	Intercede	– मध्यस्थता करना
Grandee	– एक उच्च श्रेणी दरबारी	Contrived	– कोशिश करना, उपाय निकालना
Ruinous	– नाशक, विनाशकारी	Cabal	– सत्ता लोलुप लोगों का समूह
Censure	– तीव्र आलोचना	Absurdities	– दोष
Prudence	– विवेकशीलता	Exempted	– छूट-प्राप्त
Avenues	– चौड़ी सड़क	Groves	– पेड़ों का समूह
Affectation	– बनावटी व्यवहार	Volatile	– फुर्तीला, चंचल
Prosecuting	– जारी रखना	Enterprising	– ऊर्जावान, जोशीला
Innovation	– नयापन	Sloth	– आलस्य
Repository	– संग्रहण	Agitated	– व्यथित, दु:खी

Important Questions

Questions based on the Plot of the Chapter

Q 1. Why was Balnibarbi in ruins and Lagado prosperous?

बालनीबार्बी तबाह तथा लगाडो संपन्न राज्य क्यों था?

गुलिवर लापुता से बालनीबार्बी द्वीप पर आ गया – गुलिवर उस शहर को देखकर हैरान रह गया – पूरे शहर में घर अजीब ढंग से टूटे-फूटे थे और वहाँ के लोग जंगली लगते थे – गुलिवर द्वारा इसका कारण जानने पर मुनोडी ने बताया कि चालीस साल पहले कुछ शहरवासी लापुता गए थे – खेती-बाड़ी और मरम्मत की नई तकनीकी की खोज करने लगे – मुनोडी का गाँव, जो लगाडो में था, काफी हरा-भरा तथा संपन्न था – उसने उन नए प्रयोगों को अपनाने से इंकार कर दिया – इसके लिए उसे वहाँ के लोगों का विरोध भी सहना पड़ा।

Ans. Gulliver got himself lowered down from the lowest gallery of Laputa into the continent of Balnibarbi, where he was well received by Munodi. On visiting this place, Gulliver found that the houses here were dilapidated. People went about in rags very busily with anxiety ridden expressions, labourers seemed to be hard at work with different tools. When Gulliver asked Munodi the reason for all that he saw, Munodi informed that about 40 years before, some people from Balnibarbi went up to Laputa and came back filled with ideas to reform of everything-art, science and many more. These people founded an academy in Lagado filled with professor who promised all kinds of miracles-auto ripening fruits, reduction of working hours etc. As these projects were underway. People neither had food or houses to, nor clothes to wear.

Their ideas were a complete failure and ruined everything. But the part of Lagado, which belonged to Munodi, was prosperous. It had well-built houses and well-maintained fields. It was because the Lord Munodi had no interest in innovations, he stuck to the old ways and traditional lifesytle, which saved him from utter want. Hence, heard a few others like him were looked down upon as enemies of art, common welfare and improvement of the country.

Q 2. Why was Gulliver shocked by the spectacle of Balnibarbi?

बालनीबार्बी की दशा देखकर गुलिवर स्तब्ध क्यों रह गया?

लगाडो पहुँचने के बाद गुलिवर मुनोडी के साथ बालनीबार्बी शहर को देखने निकला – वह शहर की दुर्दशा देखकर अचंभित हो गया – पूरा शहर अव्यवस्था का शिकार था – वहाँ के घर टूटे-फूटे तथा अजीब प्रकार से बने हुए थे – भूमि उपजाऊ किंतु बिना खेती की थी – लोग दुःखी तथा निराश लग रहे थे – मुनोडी के राज्य में अच्छे घर तथा भूमि उपजाऊ व हरी-भरी थी – मुनोडी का घर भी भली-भाँति निर्मित था – गुलिवर यह जानकर अचंभित हो गया कि इसके लिए वहाँ के लोग मुनोडी का उपहास उड़ाते थे।

Ans. On reaching Lagado, Gulliver visited a nearby town, called Balnibarbi. Gulliver was shocked to see the pathetic state of the city. The whole city seemed to be in a state of utter neglect. The houses were very strangely built and the people looked wild and were in rags. When he passed through one of the town gates, he saw many laboures working with several sorts of tools in the ground but were not able get success. The land was unculltivated although the soil was excellent. The people appeared depressed, miserable and unhappy. On the other hand, the estate of Munodi was well-maintained and well-developed. There he came across well built houses and well-maintained fields. The house of Munodi was also built in great taste. Gulliver paid him compliments. However, to Gulliver's shock, Munodi told how the countrymen ridiculated him for managing their affairs, the way they were being managed. This step of his had antagonised everybody.

The Royal Academy of Lagado

Gulliver visits the academy of Lagado, the capital city. He finds a person over there busy in extracting sunbeams from cucumbers. He also meets another person who is researching how to convert excrement back into food. The third person is trying to turn ice into gunpowder.

Scientist is designing a method of ploughing fields with hogs. He does so by first burying food in the ground and then letting the pigs to dig it out. A doctor tries to cure the patients by blowing air through them. He is at present reviving the dog which he has killed by way of curing it.

Experimental Part

A professor is busy with his boys working from a machine that produces random sets of woods. The professor declares that with the help of this machine anyone can write a book on philosophy or politics. Another person is busy with removing all the elements of language except nouns.

He says that this way the language will be concise and prolong lives. He says that since nouns are only things, it would be easier to carry things. Another professor tries to teach mathematics by making his students eat wafers. These wafers have mathematical proofs written on them.

Word Meaning

Sooty	– कालिख जैसा	Singed	– किनारों से जला हुआ
Vials	– दवाइयाँ रखने की छोटी शीशी	Meagre aspect	– देखने में खराब
Hermetically	– बहुत कसकर	Inclement	– तेजी (तापमान में)
Stock	– पूँजी	Intreated	– निवेदन करना
Ingenuity	– विद्वता	Conjuring	– प्रकट करना
Offence	– क्रोध का कारण	Tincture	– रंग
Scumming	– गंदगी निकालना	Ordure	– मल

5

लगाडो की शाही अकादमी

Gulliver (गुलिवर) राजधानी शहर Lagado (लगाडो) की अकादमी में जाता है। वह एक व्यक्ति को खीरों से सूर्य की किरणें निकालने में व्यस्त देखता है। वह दूसरे व्यक्ति से मिलता है जो मल को खाने में कैसे बदला जाए की खोज कर रहा है। तीसरा व्यक्ति बर्फ को गन पाउडर में बदलने की कोशिश कर रहा है।

वैज्ञानिक सुअरों द्वारा खेतों में हल चलाने के तरीके का डिजाइन बना रहा है। वह ऐसा पहले भूमि में खाना दबाकर और फिर सुअरों को इसे खोदकर निकालने द्वारा करता है। एक डॉक्टर अपने मरीजों को उनके अंदर से हवा फूँककर उनका इलाज करने की कोशिश करता है। इस समय वह एक कुत्ते को पुनर्जीवित कर रहा है, जिसे उसने उसका इलाज करने के रूप में मार दिया था।

प्रायोगिक भाग

एक प्रोफेसर अपने लड़कों के साथ एक मशीन पर कार्य करने में व्यस्त है, जो कोई भी शब्दों के सेट बनाती है। प्रोफेसर घोषणा करता है कि इस मशीन की सहायता के साथ कोई भी दर्शन या राजनीति पर एक पुस्तक लिख सकता है। दूसरा व्यक्ति भाषा की संज्ञा को छोड़कर सभी तत्वों को हटाने में व्यस्त है।

वह कहता है कि इस प्रकार भाषा संक्षिप्त रहेगी और जीवन को लंबा करेगी। वह कहता है कि संज्ञा ही सिर्फ वस्तुएँ हैं, वस्तुओं को ले जाना आसान होगा। दूसरा प्रोफेसर विद्यार्थियों को वेफर खिलाकर गणित पढ़ाने की कोशिश करता है। इन वेफर पर गणित के प्रूफ लिखे हैं।

Treatise – प्रबंध
Lamented – दुःखी होना
Fancy – पसंद करना
Diurval – प्रतिदिन
Lank – लंबा और पतला
Noxious – विषैला पदार्थ

Fraternity – बिरादरी, भाईचारा
Hues – रंग
Glutinous – चिपकने वाला
Colick – पेट से संबंधित
Orifice – शारीरिक गुहा का द्वार
Discern – पता लगाना

Important Questions

Questions based on the Plot of the Chapter

Q 1. What inferences can you draw from the experiment conducted by the Universal Artists of Lagado?

लगाडो के सार्वभौमिक कलाकार द्वारा किए गए प्रयोगों से आप क्या निष्कर्ष निकालते हैं?

सार्वभौमिक कलाकार के पास 50 आदमी काम करते थे – वे हवा को इस प्रकार वाष्पीकृत कर रहे थे कि उसे ठोस से परिवर्तित किया जाए – कुछ लोग काँच की गोलियों को तकिए में भरने के लिए मुलायम कर रहे थे – वह स्वयं भी दो महत्त्वपूर्ण कार्यों में व्यस्त था – पहला कार्य था भूसे को जमीन में बोना – दूसरा कार्य था कि गोंद, सब्जियों तथा खनिज पदार्थ के कुछ भाग को मिलाकर उसे दो भेड़ के बच्चों पर लगाना – जिससे उनके शरीर पर रुई न उग सके, इस प्रकार से वह बिना रुई वाली भेड़ का निर्माण करना चाहता था – प्रयोग/आविष्कार मूर्खतापूर्ण तथा अजीब थे – उसके द्वारा भूसे को बोने तथा बिना रुई की भेड़ पैदा करने के प्रयास व्यंग्यात्मक थे – ये सभी प्रयोग बेतुके तथा अव्यावहारिक थे।

Ans. The Universal Artist' of Lagado had been employing his thoughts for the improvement of human life for thirty years. He had two large rooms, full of wonderful curiosities and fifty men at work. Some were condensing air into a dry tangible substance, by extracting the nitre and others were softening marbles for pillows and pin-cushions. Some were petrifying the hoofs of a living horse to preserve them from foundering.

He himself was at that time busy upon two great works, the first to sow land with chaff. The other was, by a certain imposition of gums, minerals and vegetables, outwardly applied, to prevent the growth of wool upon two young lambs. So, he hoped to propagate the breed of naked sheep.

His experiments/ inventions strike the leader as very strange and also foolish. His efforts to propagate a bread of maked sheep and to sow land with chaff evoke laughter and sarcasm. These experiments were absurd and impractical.

Q 2. The projects sounded fascinating, but in reality they were funny and ridiculous, indicating the absolute stupidity of the projectors. Explain.

'वे परियोजनाएँ बेहद आकर्षक प्रतीत होती थीं, किंतु वास्तव में वे बेहूदी तथा निरर्थक थीं, जो इनकी बेवकूफी दिखाती थीं, वर्णन करें।

अकादमी ऑफ प्रोजेक्ट्स में विभिन्न परियोजनाएँ क्रियान्वित की जा रही थीं – जैसे खीरे व ककड़ी में से सूर्य की किरणें निकालना – मानवीय मल को पुनः भोजन में परिवर्तित करना – छत से प्रारंभ करके इमारत का निर्माण करना – अंधे व्यक्तियों द्वारा स्पर्श करके व गंध से रंगों को पहचानना इत्यादि – ये सारी परियोजनाएँ व्यर्थ तथा अव्यावहारिक थीं – किंतु देखने में ये बहुत आकर्षक व रुचिकर दिखती थीं – इन परियोजनाओं का कोई परिणाम नहीं निकल रहा था – क्योंकि इनका सच्चाई या वास्तविकता से कोई संबंध नहीं था – ये अद्भुत व रोमांचकारी परियोजनाएँ बेतुकी व बेकार थीं – जो कभी भी सफल नहीं हो सकती थीं – वे अपना समय, ऊर्जा तथा स्रोत इन परियोजनाओं पर व्यर्थ कर रहे थे।

Ans. In Academy of Projectors, various projects were carried out. Gulliver saw different projects like extracting sunbeams from cucumber splitting to human excreta back into food,a house built from top to bottom, blind people distinguishing colours by merely touching or smelling them, obtaining silk from cob webs, ploughing the ground by using hogs and softening marbles for pillows and pin-cushions. The scientists were busy in many more such experiments.

All these experiments seemed fascinating and interesting, but they were not getting any results from them. All those fantastic schemes were only in the air. They had no relation to the existing ground realities. Such futile and utopiam projects, however unique and ambitious they appeared, were bound to fail, as they were absurd and impractical.

They had been spending their time, energy and resources in those projects without realising the fact that those experiments could not bring out the desired results.

Q 3. Explain the new method of teaching through which most ignorant persons can write books on society low, politics, Philosophy, Poetry and mathematics etc?

पढ़ाने की उस नई विधि का वर्णन करें, जिसके द्वारा अज्ञानी व्यक्ति भी कला, साहित्य, कानून तथा राजनीति तथा गणित पर पुस्तकें लिख सकता था।

अकादमी में गुलिवर को एक ऐसे वैज्ञानिक का आविष्कार देखने को मिला, जो यह दावा करता था कि उसकी मशीन द्वारा अनपढ़ व्यक्ति भी राजनीति, कानून तथा अन्य विषयों पर पुस्तकें लिख सकता है – उसने बीस फुट बड़े वर्गाकार फ्रेम को कमरे के बीच में रखा था – उसमें तारों में अनेक अक्षर लटके हुए थे – उस फ्रेम में चालीस हैंडल थे – वैज्ञानिक के आदेश पर 36 विद्यार्थी उन हैंडल को घुमाते थे – जिसके अक्षरों की स्थिति बदल जाती थी – उन अक्षरों को मिलाकर शब्द बनाने का प्रयास किया जाता था – जोकि वाक्य का एक भाग होते थे – चार विद्यार्थियों को उन शब्दों के समूहों को लिखने के लिए कहा जाता था – इस प्रक्रिया को छः घंटे तक कई बार दोहराया जाता था – इस प्रकार टूटे-फूटे वाक्यों द्वारा कई पुस्तकें लिखी जा रही थीं – इन पुस्तकों को मिलाकर कला तथा विज्ञान की आश्चर्यजनक पुस्तकें बनाई जा सकती थीं।

Ans. In the Academy of Lagado, Gulliver came across a projector who claimed that he was devicing a method which would help the most ignorant person to write scholarly books on any subject. He had built a large frame about twenty feet square and placed in the middle of the room.

The superfies was composed of several bits of wood, which were linked together by slender wires. The bits of wood were covered on every square with paper pasted on them. On these papers were written all the words of their language, in their several modes, tenses and declensions. This frame had forty handles fixed to it. On the command of the projectors, thirty six students pulled the handles of the frame which moved the words and their position was changed.

The students were asked to read the words that would get grouped together. When three or four words seeming to be a part of sentence were found together, four students were asked to write them down.

This process was repeated several times for six hours and large volumes of books with broken sentences were compiled. These books were later to be pieced together to give the world wonderful books on arts and science.

Questions based on the Character Sketch

Q 4. Comment on the projectors and their hope of success. Why did they fail to realise their mistake though they had been busy in their projects for a long time and that too, without any success?

अकादमी के प्रोजेक्टर्स तथा उनकी सफलता पाने की आशा पर टिप्पणी करें। वे अपनी गलतियों पर वर्षों से कार्य कर रहे थे और उन्हें इनमें सफलता भी नहीं मिल रही थी।

लगाडो की अकादमी में अनेक प्रोजेक्टर्स अनेक प्रयोगों में व्यस्त थे – एक वैज्ञानिक खीरों से सूर्य किरणें निकालने का प्रयत्न कर रहा था – दूसरा वैज्ञानिक मनुष्य के मल-मूत्र को फिर से खाने के असली स्वरूप में बदलने का प्रयत्न कर रहा था – एक वैज्ञानिक बर्फ को बारूद में परिवर्तित करना चाहता था – एक वैज्ञानिक मकड़ी के जालों से रेशम प्राप्त करने का प्रयत्न कर रहा था – ये वैज्ञानिक इन परियोजनाओं पर कई सालों से कार्य कर रहे थे – ये परियोजनाएँ ऐसी थीं, जो असफल ही हो सकती थीं, सफल नहीं – क्योंकि वे वैज्ञानिक अपने व्यावहारिक ज्ञान का उपयोग नहीं कर रहे थे – वे विज्ञान के नियमों व विचारधाराओं का आँख मूँदकर प्रयोग कर रहे थे – अतः उनके यह प्रयोग निरर्थक तथा बेकार थे।

Ans. In Lagado, Gulliver paid a visit to the Academy of Projectors. There he met the warden and a number of projectors in charge of various projects. He met a bearded man who had been engaged for eight years upon a project. He was trying to extract sunbeams out of cucumbers. Another man at the Academy had been employed for a long time on a project. It aimed at restoring human excreta to its original food. One of the projectors was trying to calcine ice into gun-powder. A most ingenious architect had deviced a new method of building houses.

He began at the roof and worked downwards to the foundation. Another projector was trying to obtain silk from the cobwebs. Apart from these, many more projects were carried out by the projectors. Those projectors had been working on these projects for many years and were very hopeful that one day they would get success. But they failed to realise that these projects lacked practical knowledge, commonsense and a general approach. They had no relation to the existing ground realities. They did not applied the laws of science in appropriate way. Most of the projects were improbable and impractical. These projects ranged from absurd to sheer insane. The projectors accepted anything in the name of science. Therefore, they were not getting success in these projects.

Depressing Political Projects

Gulliver meets some political scientists whom he finds quite insane. They have proposed that administrators should be chosen for their wisdom, talent and skill. Their ability and virtue should be rewarded. Ministers should be chosen for their love of public good. These political scientists are studying issues of the government. One professor claims that woman should be taxed according to their beauty and skill at dressing. Another professor claims that conspiracies against the government could be discovered by studying the excrement of subjects. Thus all those scientists and professors are mad. Gulliver feels bored and wants to return to England.

निराशाजनक राजनैतिक परियोजनाएँ

Gulliver (गुलिवर) को कुछ राजनैतिक वैज्ञानिक मिलते हैं, जिन्हें वह पागल पाता है। उन्होंने सुझाव दिया है कि प्रबंधकों को उनकी बुद्धिमत्ता, गुण और निपुणता के लिए चुनना चाहिए। उनके गुण और योग्यता का ईनाम मिलना चाहिए। मंत्रियों को उनके जनता की भलाई के प्रति प्यार के लिए चुनना चाहिए। ये राजनैतिक-वैज्ञानिक सरकार की समस्याएँ पढ़ रहे हैं। एक प्रोफेसर कहता है कि महिलाओं पर उनकी सुंदरता और कपड़े पहनने की निपुणता के अनुसार टैक्स लगाना चाहिए। दूसरा प्रोफेसर कहता है कि जनता के मल को पढ़कर सरकार के प्रति षड्यंत्रों को खोजना चाहिए। इस प्रकार सभी वैज्ञानिक और प्रोफेसर पागल हैं। गुलिवर बोर महसूस करता है और वापिस इंग्लैंड लौटना चाहता है।

Word Meaning

Visionary	– दूरदर्शिता	Remedies	– उपाय, उपचार
Licentiousness	– अनियंत्रित कामुक व्यवहार	Redundant	– अनिच्छुक
Ebullient	– जोश से भरा	Peccant	– अपमान
Purulent	– पीपदार	Maladies	– रोग
Apothecaries	– दवा बेचने वाला	Lenitives	– प्रशामक
Aperitives	– मद्य पेय	Palliatives	– दर्दनाशक

Important Questions

Questions based on the Plot of the Chapter

Q 1. What were the various projects going on at the political school? How were they different from those at the schools of language and mathematics as regard to their aspects or success?

राजनैतिक स्कूल में कौन-से नए प्रोजेक्ट चल रहे थे? वे प्रोजेक्ट्स किस प्रकार भाषा के स्कूल तथा गणित के स्कूल से भिन्न थे?

राजनैतिक विद्यालय में गुलिवर ने देखा कि सम्राटों को अपनी बुद्धि व समझ के अनुसार अपने चापलूस चुनने के लिए मनाया जा रहा था – राजनैतिक बीमारियों का शारीरिक बीमारियों की भाँति इलाज किया जा रहा था – एक चिकित्सक सांसदों की बहस के दौरान उनका परीक्षण करे – उन्हें उनके अनुसार दवाईयाँ देकर मानसिक रूप से चुस्त रखा जाए – दो विरोधी पार्टियों के सदस्यों के मध्य समझौता कराने के लिए उन सदस्यों के मस्तिष्क को दो भागों में काटकर अलग-अलग व्यक्तियों के मस्तिष्क के साथ शल्य चिकित्सा द्वारा जोड़ दिया जाए – इससे वे एक-दूसरे के विचारों को भली प्रकार समझ सकेंगे – औरतों की सुंदरता तथा पहनने के तरीकों पर कर लगाया जाए।

Ans. In the political school, Gulliver saw projectors persuading emperor choose favourites on the basis of their intellect and calibre. Another project was regarding giving the same treatment for physical as well as political ailment. So, it was decided that physicians should monitor the politicians during the senate meeting and feel their pulse and administer medicines to keep them mentally fit. These ministers should be kicked, pulled up and shaken up so that they remember to fulfil their promises. These reminders should be given to them repeatedly.

A method to bring about a reconciliation between the views of two opposition parties was also developed. The brains of different members should be cut into halves and then the two halves should be surgically put together. This would help them understand each other's views and come to a mutual understanding. New methods of taxation were suggested.

One was to impose taxes on vices and follies of an individual. This tax was to be calculated by the neighbours. Wit, valour and politeness among men and beauty and sense of dressing among women was also to be taxed. These were some schemes which were carried out by the projectors of political school.

Gulliver's visit to the Island of Glubbdubdrib

Gulliver leaves Lagado and arrives at Maldonada. No ship is ready for sail. Gulliver takes a short voyage in Glubbdubdrib. To the North of Lagado is situated the island of Luggnagg, not far South-East of Japan. Gulliver decides to visit Luggnagg, sail for Japan and then head for Europe. Gulliver hires a guide to assist him to the island of Luggnagg. He arrives at the port city Maldonada, but to his shock, no ship is bound for Luggnagg. Gulliver has to wait for a month.

Accompanied by the two companions, Gulliver reaches the island about 11 am. They seek the permission to enter the palace and are received by the Governor. The Governor inquires Gulliver about some of his adventurous voyages.

गुलिवर की ग्लबड्बड्रिब द्वीप की यात्रा

Gulliver (गुलिवर) Lagado (लगाडो) से रवाना होकर Maldonada (माल्डोनाडा) पहुँच जाता है। कोई भी जहाज यात्रा हेतु तैयार नहीं था। गुलिवर एक छोटी समुद्री यात्रा करके Glubbdubdrib (ग्लबडबड्रिब) पहुँचता है। लगाडो के उत्तर में Luggnagg (लगनैग) नामक द्वीप स्थित है, जोकि Japan (जापान) के दक्षिण-पूर्व से अधिक दूरी पर नहीं है। गुलिवर लगनैग की यात्रा करने, जहाज द्वारा जापान की यात्रा करने तथा फिर यूरोप जाने का निर्णय लेता है। लगनैग द्वीप पर स्वयं की सहायता हेतु गुलिवर एक पथ प्रदर्शक को किराए पर रख लेता है। वह माल्डोनाडा बंदरगाह पर पहुँच जाता है, परंतु उसे धक्का लगा कि लगनैग जाने के लिए कोई भी जहाज तैयार नहीं था। गुलिवर को एक माह तक प्रतीक्षा करनी पड़ी।

दो साथियों के साथ गुलिवर प्रात: लगभग 11 बजे द्वीप पर पहुँचा। Palace (राजमहल) में प्रवेश करने हेतु उन्होंने अनुमति ली तथा Governor (राज्यपाल) ने उनका स्वागत किया। राज्यपाल ने गुलिवर से उसकी साहसिक समुद्री यात्रा के विषय में पूछा।

Word Meaning

Alliance	– संधि करना	Bark	– तैरने वाला जहाज
Profound	– तीव्र	Obeisances	– सम्मान से सिर झुकाना
Spectres	– भूत जैसी आकृतियाँ	Knot	– एक समूह
Veneration	– आदर	Consummate	– (यहाँ) परिपूर्ण, सटीक
Interpidity	– निर्भिकता	Sextumuirate	– छः का समूह

Important Questions

Questions based on the Plot of the Chapter

Q 1. Gulliver wanted to visit Luggnagg, but he visited Glubbdubdrib. Why?

गुलिवर लगनैग जाना चाहता था, किंतु वह ग्लबडबड्रिब चला गया। क्यों?

गुलिवर वापस अपने देश जाना चाहता था – रास्ते में वह लगनैग तथा जापान होकर जाना चाहता था – जापान के शासक तथा लगनैग के सम्राट के मध्य एक संधि हुई थी, जिसके अनुसार वे एक-दूसरे के द्वीप पर आ-जा सकते थे – अतः गुलिवर माल्डोनाडा के बंदरगाह तक पहुँचा–उस बंदरगाह पर लगनैग के लिए कोई जहाज नहीं मिला – चूँकि लगनैग के लिए जहाज एक महीने से पहले नहीं तैयार होगा – इसलिए उसके एक परिचित व्यक्ति ने सुझाया कि वह इतने में ग्लबडबड्रिब का भ्रमण कर ले – जोकि दक्षिण-पश्चिम में स्थित था।

Ans. Gulliver wanted to return to his own country but before it, he wanted to visit the great island of Luggnagg. This island of Luggnagg stands South-Eastwards of Japan, about a hundred leagues distant. This is a strict alliance between the Japanese emperor and the Emperor of Luggnagg which allows frequent opportunities of sailing from one island to the other. So, Gulliver determined to go to this island as well as to Japan, in order to return to Europe. As he reached the port of Maldonada, he was informed that there was no ship bound for Luggnagg and there was no hope of getting one for a good length of time.

Since he had to wait for a month, he was suggested by an acquaintance of his to take a trip to the little island of Glubbdubdrib, the island of magicians. He even offered to give him company along with another friend of his. So, Gulliver, with his two companions, started for the little island of Glubbdubdrib, about five leagues off to the South-West.

Meets the Renowned from the Grave

Having conversed with many celebrities including Alexander the Great, Hannibal, Julius Caesar, famous for their wit and learning, Gulliver gets to meet the ancient Greek poet Homer and the philosopher Aristotle. He also comes to meet the French philosophers Ren Descartes and Pierre Gassendi.

विख्यात मृत व्यक्तियों से मिलना

अनेक विख्यात व्यक्तियों; जैसे– Alexander (अलेक्जेंडर) महान्, Hannibal (हनीबाल), Julius Caesar (जूलियस सीजर) जो अपने ज्ञान एवं वाक्पटुता हेतु विख्यात थे, से संवाद करने के पश्चात् गुलिवर प्राचीन Greek (ग्रीक) कवि Homer (होमर) तथा दार्शनिक Aristotle (अरस्तू) से मिलने का अवसर प्राप्त करता है। वह French Philosophers Ren Descartes (फ्रांसीसी दार्शनिक रेनी देकार्ते) एवं Pierre Gassendi (पियरे गैसेंडी) से भी मिलता है।

Gulliver also Talks to Most of the Emperors of Rome

He sees the generation of the royal houses of Europe and discovers a mixture of many commoners like a barber, an abbot and the two fiddlers. Then he meets those who died recently. But Gulliver is depressed.

गुलिवर का रोम के अधिकांश शासकों के साथ वार्तालाप करना

वह Europe (यूरोप) के शाही परिवारों की पीढ़ियों को देखता है तथा उसे कई सामान्य नागरिक; जैसे-एक नाई, एक सारंगी बजाने वाले तथा दो महंत नजर आए। इसके पश्चात् वह उन लोगों से मिलता है, जिनकी मृत्यु हाल ही में हुई थी। परंतु गुलिवर निराश हो गया।

Word Meaning

Cornelier	– अधिक आकर्षक	Visage	– चेहरा
Meagre	– पतला या कमजोर	Lank	– लंबा
Prevailed	– मनाना	Dunces	– कम दिमाग वाला बेवकूफ व्यक्ति
Palatable	– सहमत	Zealous	– जोशीला
Out of vogue	– प्रचलन से बाहर	Helot	– कोई भी दास
Grievous	– तकलीफ देह	Diadems	– रत्नों से जड़ा मुकुट
Fiddles	– वायलिन बजाने वाला	Spruce	– आकर्षक ढंग से
Veneration	– आदर	Knaves	– धोखेबाज
Scrofulous	– नैतिक रूप से बीमार	Lackeys	– पुरुष नौकर
Gamester	– जुआरी	Counsel	– सुझाव देना
Piety	– धर्मपरायणता	Atheists	– ईश्वर को न मानने वाला
Chastity	– पवित्रता	Bawd	– वेश्यालय की देखभाल करने वाला
Buffoons	– जोकर	Anecdotes	– छोटी मनोरंजक कहानियाँ
Whore	– वेश्या	Restive	– बेचैन
Clog	– रुकावट	Infancy	– बदनामी
Perjury	– झूठी गवाही	Oppression	– उत्पीड़न, दमन

Important Questions

Questions based on the Plot of the Chapter

Q 1. What shocking facts are highlighted through Gulliver's conversation with Aristotle and Homer?

अरस्तू तथा होमर से बातचीत करके गुलिवर को कौन-से आश्चर्यजनक तथ्य पता लगे?

गुलिवर की प्रार्थना पर गवर्नर होमर व अरस्तू तथा उनके समीक्षकों को बुलाता था – दोनों ही अत्यधिक प्रभावशाली व्यक्तित्व के थे – वे समीक्षक जो उनकी आलोचना करते थे उनका सामना करने की हिम्मत नहीं कर पा रहे थे – दोनों महान् व्यक्ति उन आलोचकों को नहीं जानते थे – होमर को डिडिमस तथा अस्टेथियस में कुछ भी महान् नहीं लगा – अरस्तू को भी ये आलोचक बेवकूफ लगे – आधुनिक दर्शनशास्त्री डेस्कार्ट तथा गैसेंडी को भी बुलाया गया – अरस्तू ने प्राकृतिक दर्शनशास्त्र में अपनी गलती मानी – उन्होंने आधुनिक दर्शनशास्त्र में कई कमियाँ निकालीं और कहा कि यह सभी आधुनिक सोच पर भी लागू होता है – होमर व अरस्तू ने स्वयं को सबसे महान् सिद्ध कर दिया।

Ans. At Gulliver's request, the Governor summoned Homer and Aristotle along with their critics. Both great personalities appeared very exclusive and impressive. None of the two seemed to know anyone of them. Homer saw no genius at all in poets like Didymus and Eustathius.

Aristotle too considered all these commentators and critics to be great fools. Descartes and Gassendi were also be summoned who were modern philosophers. Gulliver was shocked when Aristotle admitted his own mistakes in natural philosophy. Philosophers like Gassendi were criticised by him and he predicted that their works would not stand the test of time as their theories were hollow and shallow. He also pointed out that the system of nature would always vary from age to age.

Gulliver realised that the talent of these two grand masters (Aristotle and Homer) was unmatchable. These philosophers were morally sound as they taught everything with morality and honesty.

Q 2. Sum up Gulliver's conversation with the dead and his reaction. What else did he see?

गुलिवर द्वारा मृत व्यक्ति से वार्तालाप तथा उसकी प्रतिक्रिया को संक्षिप्त करें। उसने और क्या देखा?

आत्माओं से बातचीत करते समय गुलिवर को कई आश्चर्यजनक तथ्य पता चले – उसे बताया गया कि ईमानदार, वफादार तथा कर्त्तव्यनिष्ठ व्यक्तियों को न तो कभी सम्मानित किया गया और न ही उनका इतिहास में कोई उल्लेख है – बल्कि कई बार उन्हें खलनायक, धूर्त तथा देशद्रोही के रूप में दिखाया गया – उन्हें या तो मार दिया गया या उन्होंने अपना जीवन गरीबी तथा शर्म में गुजारा – जहाज के एक कमांडर ने युद्ध में अपना इकलौता बेटा खो दिया था – वह युद्ध में बहादुरी तथा ईमानदारी से लड़ा – किंतु उस पर अपने कर्त्तव्य की उपेक्षा का आरोप लगाया गया – इस पर उस निराश व्यक्ति ने आत्महत्या कर ली – गुलिवर ने मृत तथा जीवित व्यक्तियों की तुलना करते हुए पाया कि वर्तमान समय में लोग इतने नीचे गिर चुके हैं कि वे अपने वोट बेच देते हैं – चुनावों में हेरफेर करते हैं – सिर्फ धन कमाने के लिए लोगों का नैतिक पतन हो चुका है – वह यह जानकर निराश व दुःखी हुआ।

Ans. While conversing with the spirits, Gulliver came to know many shocking facts and revelations. He was informed that the services of the loyal, sincere and conscientious were neither rewarded nor mentioned in history. Rather at times, they were represented as the villain, rogues and traitors. They were either sentenced to death or they died in poverty and disgrace.

A commander of a ship who lost his only son in the war and who fought very bravely and sincerely, was charged with neglect of duty. The poor man was so shocked by this that he retired to a poor farm far away from Rome and ended his life there. On the other hand, many officers got ill, deserved promotions.

On comparing the dead with the living, Gulliver concluded that in the present time, people had stooped so low as to sell off their votes, manipulate the elections and resort to many corrupt practices just to grab some money. The people were morally degenerated. This had made him disgusted and disappointed.

Questions based on the Character Sketch

Q 3. Draw a character sketch of Aristotle and Homer, based on your reading of the current chapter.

पाठ के अध्ययन के आधार पर अरस्तू तथा होमर का चरित्र चित्रण करें।

अरस्तू व होमर प्राचीन दर्शनशास्त्री थे – होमर लंबी कद-काठी का था, जो बिल्कुल सीधा चलता था – उसकी आँखें तेज व प्रभावित करने वाली थीं – अरस्तू झुककर चलता था और छड़ी का प्रयोग करता था – उसका चेहरा लंबा तथा बाल लंबे व पतले थे – उसकी आवाज खोखली थी – अरस्तू ने बहुत नम्रता से अपनी प्राकृतिक दर्शनशास्त्र की गलती मान ली – वह एक दूरदर्शी था तथा स्क्रोटस व रैमस की आलोचना की – जबकि होमर ने डिडिमस तथा अस्टेथियस से विनम्रता से बात की – अरस्तू ने साबित कर दिया कि वह सबसे महान् है, क्योंकि उसने आधुनिक दर्शनशास्त्र में भी कमियाँ निकालीं – उसने बताया कि यह सभी आधुनिक विचारों पर भी लागू होता है।

Ans. Aristotle and Homer were ancient philosophers. Homer was taller and an attractive person who walked very erect and his eyes were very quick and piercing. Aristotle stooped much and made use of a staff. His face was thin. His hair were long and thin and his voice was hollow. He was a great philosopher, was humble though being so learned. He admitted his mistakes in natural philosophy. He was a visionary and very strongly criticised Scrotus and Ramus. While Homer was very polite to Didymus and Eustathius.

He found they wanted a genius to enter into the spirit of a poet. Aristotle proved himself to be the greatest by showing shortcomings of modern philosophy and by predicting the same fate for the current favourites. None of the two seemed to know the modern critics. The talent of none of the poet's critics and philosopher matched that of these two great personalities.

Introduction

Gulliver leaves Glubbdubdrib, the land of black magicians. He returns to Maldonada. He reaches Luggnagg. There he is captivated. He is sent for to court. He comes across stupid customs at court. Finally, he is liked by the emperor and stays there for three months.

Gulliver Reaches Luggnagg

He arrives in Luggnagg on April 21, 1708. Gulliver starts speaking to a custom officer in Luggnagg, who examines him very strictly. The officer speaks to Gulliver in the language of Balnibarbi, easily spoken and understood there.

Gulliver pretends to be Dutch, concealing the identity of his country, as the Dutch are the only Europeans permitted to enter into that kingdom.

Impractical Customs at Court

Eventually, Gulliver is granted an interview with the emperor of Luggnagg. Gulliver has to follow the local custom of licking the dust before the emperor footstool. The floor is scattered with dust for the person supposed to have powerful enemies at the court and when emperor wishes to kill someone, the floor is sprinkled a brown powder. The person who licks the floor, dies in twenty four hours.

Word Meaning

Shoals	– छिछला पानी	Treachery	– विश्वासघात
Inadvertence	– लापरवाही	Plausible	– विश्वसनीय
Sentry	– संतरी, पहरेदार	Retinue	– नौकर-चाकर
Strewed	– फैला देना	Crammed	– व्यवस्थित

9

परिचय

Gulliver (गुलिवर) जादूगरों की धरती Glubbdubdrib (ग्लबडबड्रिब) को छोड़कर चला जाता है। वह वापस Maldonada (माल्डोनाडा) पहुँचता है। वह लगनैग पहुँचता है। वहाँ उसे बंदी बना लिया जाता है। उसे Court (न्यायालय) भेजा जाता है। उसे न्यायालय के मूर्खतापूर्ण नियम पता चल जाते हैं। अंततः सम्राट को वह पसंद आ जाता है तथा वह तीन माह तक वहाँ रहता है।

गुलिवर लगनैग पहुँचता है

वह 21 अप्रैल, 1708 को लगनैग पहुँचता है। गुलिवर एक सीमा शुल्क अधिकारी से बात करने लगता है, जो गहन रूप से उसकी जाँच करता है। अधिकारी गुलिवर से Balnibarbi (बालनीबार्बी) भाषा में बात करने लगा जो वहाँ भली-भाँति बोली तथा समझी जाती थी।

गुलिवर स्वयं के डच होने का दिखावा करता है तथा अपने देश की पहचान छुपाता है, क्योंकि उस राज्य में प्रवेश की अनुमति यूरोपीय देशों में मात्र डच लोगों को ही थी।

अव्यावहारिक रीति-रिवाज

अंततः गुलिवर को लगनैग के सम्राट से बात करने की अनुमति मिल जाती है। गुलिवर को सम्राट के सिंहासन के सामने की धूल चाटने के स्थानीय रिवाज का पालन करना पड़ा। ऐसे व्यक्ति के आने पर जो राज्य के लिए शक्तिशाली शत्रु होता था, जमीन पर अधिक मात्रा में कचरा बिखेर दिया जाता था और जब सम्राट किसी व्यक्ति को मारना चाहता था तो जमीन पर एक भूरे रंग का पाउडर छिड़क दिया जाता था। जो व्यक्ति जमीन को चाटता था, चौबीस घंटों में उसकी मृत्यु हो जाती थी।

Infallibly – बिना विफल हुए
Clemency – क्षमा, दया
Incurring – अनुभव करना
Whip – चाबुक से मारना
Maliciously – घृणास्पद
Digression – मुख्य बात से भटकना
High Chamberlain – राजमहल का बड़ा अधिकारी

Important Questions

Questions based on the Plot of the Chapter

Q 1. Describe Gulliver's journey from Maldonada to court.

गुलिवर की माल्डोनाडा से दरबार तक की यात्रा का वर्णन कीजिए।

↗ ग्लबडबड्रिब के गवर्नर से विदा लेकर गुलिवर माल्डोनाडा पहुँचा – लगनैग के लिए जहाज पंद्रह दिन बाद जाना था – कस्टम अधिकारी से गुलिवर ने विस्तृत रूप से पूछताछ की – दरबार का आदेश आने तक गुलिवर को बंदी बनाकर रखा गया – इसके लिए गुलिवर को रखने के लिए घर दिया गया – गुलिवर को दरबार के आदेश मिल जाते हैं – गुलिवर के आगमन की सूचना देने के लिए एक संदेशवाहक पहले ही भेज दिया गया था।

Ans. Gulliver took leave of the Governor of Glubbdubdrib and reached Maldonada. After waiting for a fortnight, a ship was ready to sail for Luggnagg. On landing, some of the sailors informed a custom officer that he was a stranger and a great traveller. The custom-officer interrogated him thoroughly.

Gulliver gave him a brief account of his adventures but introduced himself as *a* Dutch as he knew that Dutch were the only Europeans permitted to enter Japan. The officer proposed to confine him for a fortnight till he received orders from the court.

Gulliver was taken to a lodging where he was treated with great humanity. He was visited by many people. Gulliver hired an interpreter who was well versed in the language of Luggnagg as well as Maldonada. With the help of this interpreter, Gulliver conversed with the visitors.

Gulliver requested to take his interpreter along with him. They were given a mule each. A messenger was sent in advance to inform the emperor about Gulliver's arrival.

Q 2. Describe the customs of court and comment as to how ridiculous and irrelevant they sound to you, despite their careful application.

दरबार में प्रचलित रिवाजों पर टिप्पणी करें, वे आपको कैसे अर्थहीन लगे?

गुलिवर को लगनैग के सम्राट से मिलने की अनुमति मिल गई – इसके लिए उसे पेट के बल लेटकर रेंगते हुए तथा फर्श को चाटते हुए जाना था – गुलिवर के अजनबी होने के कारण फर्श को साफ रखा जाता है – अन्य दरबारियों को धूल से भरे फर्श को चाटना पड़ता है – किसी को मारने के लिए फर्श पर भूरे रंग के जहरीले पाउडर का छिड़काव कर दिया जाता था – सम्राट के सिंहासन के पास पहुँचकर गुलिवर घुटनों के बल बैठ गया – सम्राट लोगों को अपने सम्मान में झुकाकर नीचा दिखाना चाहता था तथा उसे चापलूसी और तारीफ भरे शब्द पसंद थे।

Ans. Gulliver had got the permission to meet the Luggnaggian emperor. Before he presented himself in the royal court, he was ordered to follow the Luggnaggian custom of appearing before the emperor, according to which, he was to crawl on his belly and keep on licking the floor as he advanced.

Since Gulliver was a foreigner, he was given the liberty of crawling on and licking a well-cleaned floor. Otherwise, the ordinary lord had to lick the floor so full of dust that they could not utter even a single word in the emperor presence.

They were not even permitted to spit or wipe their mouth in his presence. At times, the emperor got the floor covered with a poisonous brown powder, when he wished to put someone to death.

When Gulliver reached within four yards of the throne, he sat on his knees. According to the custom, he had to strike his forehead seven times against the floor and had to wish the emperor a very long life. These customs were very funny and absurd. It showed that the emperor expect all the people lower down in order to bow to them. They expected sweet words of flattery and praise from them.

Introduction

Gulliver describes the immortals or Struldbrugs. Gulliver is excited to know about their immortality, but having come to know many a negative point of immortals, he is depressed. Gulliver is lamenting their fate.

The Struldbrug or Immortal

The Luggnaggians inform Gulliver about a sort of people who never die. They are Struldbrugs or immortals. A Struldbrug is a child born with a mark on its forehead, over its left eyebrow. This very mark indicates that the child is immortal.

Gulliver's Plans If He was an Immortal

Gulliver is inquired as to what he would do in case he is an immortal. Gulliver's answers are very exciting and zealous. He would make abundant money, invest it and save it. He would try to be the richest man in the kingdom. He would learn everything.

Word Meaning

Counternanced	– समर्थक	Appellation	– शीर्षक
Extravagant	– खर्चीला	Rapture	– उत्साहित
Apprehensions	– चिंताएँ	Libertine	– अनैतिक
Opinionated	– दृढ़ विचारों वाला	Dictates	– आज्ञा देना
Discourse	– वार्तालाप	Eloquent	– बोलने में माहिर
Copious	– अत्यधिक	Procure	– हासिल करना
Oracle	– भविष्यवाणी करने वाला	Fortified	– सीधा करना

10

परिचय

Gulliver (गुलिवर) अमर लोगों अथवा Struldbrugs (स्ट्रल्डब्रग्स) के विषय में बताता है। गुलिवर उनके अमरत्व के विषय में जानकर अत्यंत प्रसन्न होता है, परंतु अमर व्यक्तियों के विभिन्न नकारात्मक पक्षों को जानकर उसे अत्यंत निराशा होती है। गुलिवर उन व्यक्तियों के भाग्य पर दु:खी होता है।

स्ट्रल्डब्रग्स अथवा अमर लोग

लगनैग के निवासी गुलिवर को एक ऐसी प्रजाति के विषय में बताते हैं, जिसके व्यक्ति कभी मृत नहीं होते। ये स्ट्रल्डब्रग्स या अमर लोग थे। एक स्ट्रल्डब्रग्स बच्चे के जन्म के साथ ही उसकी बाईं भौंह के ऊपर मस्तक पर एक निशान पाया जाता था। इस निशान से इस बात की पुष्टि होती थी कि बच्चा अमर होगा।

गुलिवर यदि अमर होता तो उसकी योजनाएँ

गुलिवर से पूछा जाता है कि यदि वह अमर हो जाता तो वह क्या करता। गुलिवर के उत्तर अत्यंत उत्साहपूर्ण तथा उत्तेजक थे। वह अत्यधिक धन कमाता, विनियोग करता तथा बचत भी करता। वह साम्राज्य का सर्वाधिक धनी व्यक्ति बनने का प्रयास करता। वह सब कुछ सीख लेता।

Contemporaries	– समकक्ष	Degeneracy	– अमरत्व
Barbarity	– क्रूरता	Sublunary	– सांसारिक
Imbecility	– बेवकूफी	Retreat	– वापस लेना
Contrived	– कल्पना करना	Infirmities	– कमजोरी, बीमारी
Peevish	– चिड़चिड़े ढंग से	Covetous	– लालची
Morose	– दु:खी, नाखुश	Impotent	– शक्तिहीन
Repine	– पछतावा	Dotage	– बुढ़ापा

Important Questions

Questions based on the Plot of the Chapter

Q 1. Who were the Struldbrugs? How was their birth reacted to?

स्ट्रल्डब्रग्स कौन थे? उनके जन्म पर क्या प्रतिक्रिया होती थी?

लगनैग के लोगों से बात करते समय गुलिवर को स्ट्रल्डब्रग्स या अमर व्यक्तियों के बारे में पता चला – स्ट्रल्डब्रग्स ऐसे व्यक्ति थे, जो नश्वर माता-पिता की संतान थे – इन्हें निरंतर जीवन का श्राप मिला था – ऐसे व्यक्ति कभी-कभी पैदा होते थे – जन्म के समय इनके माथे पर बाईं ओर एक निशान होता था – इनके विवाह टूट जाते थे – इनकी संपत्ति इनके बच्चों के पास चली जाती थी – ये न ही कोई नौकरी कर सकते थे, न ही जमीन खरीद सकते, न ही गवाही दे सकते थे – वे मृत्यु के लिए तरसते थे – वृद्धावस्था की असक्षमताएँ उनका जीवन भयावह बना देती थीं।

Ans. One day, Gulliver was chatting with some Luggnaggian with the help of his interpreter. He was asked if he had ever met a Struldbrug or an immortal. Then he was informed that Struldbrugs were human being who were born to normal, mortal parents, with the curse of living an eternal life. Such people were born occasionally and the entire kingdom had hardly a few thousands of such immortals of both sexes.

A child, born with a mark on his forehead, over his left eyebrow, is considered as immortal. By the time the child is twelve years, the mark grows bigger and changes its colour into green. Their deathless life was full of pessimism, pain, boredom and monotony. At the age of eighty, they started losing interest in life, even the society started ignoring them.

Their property was inherited by their children and the law took them to be as good as dead. They could not do any job and they could neither purchased land or take leases, nor be a witness in any case.

They yearned to die as the infirmities of old age made their lives a horrifying experience. They lived a dejected and neglected life.

Q 2. What would Gulliver do if he was an immortal?

अमर होने पर गुलिवर क्या करना चाहता था?

गुलिवर अपने अमर होने पर अपनी संपूर्ण योजना के बारे में बताता है – अगर वह अमर होता तो वह सबसे धनी व्यक्ति बनता – वह सबसे अधिक विद्वान् व्यक्ति बनने की कोशिश करता – वह समाज से भ्रष्टाचार समाप्त करने, मानवीय मूल्यों के हनन को रोकने की भी कोशिश करता – वह नए देशों के राजनैतिक बदलावों, नई खोजों पर भी नजर रखता – वह नदियों में बदलाव, बड़े शहरों का विनाश तथा गाँवों का विकास भी देखता – इसके अतिरिक्त वह खगोलीय पिंडों के परिवर्तन व धूमकेतु के आवागमन को भी जानता – इस प्रकार गुलिवर अपने कभी न समाप्त होने वाले जीवन का उपयोग करता।

Ans. When Gulliver came to know about Struldbrugs, he felt very excited. He could not believe that certain human beings never faced the inevitable fact of death. He would amuse himself with the question of what he would do if he was a Struldbrug. Gulliver replied that he would spend the first two hundred years to become the wealthiest man of the world. He would work hard to become the most learned person.

Apart from it, he would keep not only a record of all the events and happenings of the state but also make a note of all the changes in customs, fashions and language. He would become a living dtorehouse of knowledge and wisdom. He would not marry after the age of sixty and devote his life in aparting knowledge and good values to the young people. He would form a group of Struldbrugs and provide them financial help, if require. With of help of these companions, he would try to put a check on corrupt practices and corruption in the society.

He would instruct the citizen of his country against the degeneration of human nature and provide them valuable guidance. He would also keep any eye on the political changes and discoveries of new countries. He would observe the changing course of the rivers, destruction of grand cities and development of villages. Apart from it, he would also see the changes in the celestial bodies and the movement of comet. In this way, he wanted to utilize his never ending life.

11

Gulliver Leaves Luggnagg

Gulliver leaves Luggnagg. From Luggnagg he sails to Japan, from Japan to Amsterdam and from Amsterdam to England. Gulliver is offered an employment by the Luggnaggian emperor in the court, but as Gulliver is missing home, he is firm to return to England. The emperor gives him a license to leave, a letter of recommendation and a generous gift of 444 pieces of gold, accompanied by a precious red diamond. He uses the letter of recommendation given by the Luggnaggian emperor to get an audience with the emperor of Japan. The emperor and Gulliver converse with each other in Dutch. Gulliver introduces himself as a Dutch merchant who has to head to Nangasac.

गुलिवर लगनैग छोड़ देता है

Gulliver (गुलिवर) Luggnagg (लगनैग) द्वीप छोड़ देता है। वह लगनैग से Japan (जापान) तक जापान से Amsterdam (एम्सटर्डम) तक तथा एम्सटर्डम से England (इंग्लैंड) तक जहाज यात्रा करता है। लगनैग के सम्राट ने गुलिवर को न्यायालय में एक नौकरी का प्रस्ताव दिया, परंतु गुलिवर अपने घर को याद कर रहा था। अत: वह इंग्लैंड लौटने हेतु दृढ़ था। सम्राट उसे द्वीप छोड़ने की अनुमति सिफारिशी पत्र एवं उपहारस्वरूप एक बहुमूल्य Red Diamond (लाल हीरे) के साथ-साथ 444 सोने के सिक्के देता है। वह लगनैग के सम्राट के द्वारा दिए गए सिफारिशी पत्र का प्रयोग जापान के सम्राट से मुलाकात करने में करता है। सम्राट एवं गुलिवर आपस में Dutch Language (डच भाषा) में बात करते हैं। गुलिवर अपना परिचय वहाँ एक डच व्यापारी के रूप में देता है, जिसे Nangasac (नांगासाक) जाना था।

Word Meaning

Censure – आलोचना
Perpetual – निरंतर
Conduct – साथ जाना
Transact – पूरा करना
Condescend – गरिमापूर्ण
Transcribe – बार-बार लिखना
Pressed – दबाव बनाना
Straight – पानी जाने का संकरा रास्ता
Conducted – वापस ले लेना
Scruple – झिझक होना

Important Questions

Questions based on the Plot of the Chapter

Q 1. Describe Gulliver's meeting with the emperor of Japan.

गुलिवर की जापान के राजा से भेंट का वर्णन करें।

जापान के एक्सेमोस्ची बंदरगाह पर गुलिवर का स्वागत हुआ – उसने लगनैग के सम्राट का पत्र कस्टम अधिकारी को दिखाया – वे उस पर लगी सील को पहचानते थे – उसे घोड़ा गाड़ी में येडो ले जाया गया – जहाँ उसे जापान के सम्राट से मिलने का अवसर मिला – वहाँ एक भव्य समारोह के बाद उस सिफारिशी पत्र को खोला गया – गुलिवर ने स्वयं को डच व्यापारी बताया तथा सम्राट ने उसे नांगासाक पहुँचाने के लिए कहा – उसने यीशु के क्रॉस को पैरों से कुचलने की प्रथा से स्वयं को अलग रखने को कहा – जापान का सम्राट अत्यधिक आश्चर्यचकित हुआ।

Ans. Gulliver was given a respectable welcome when he landed at the port of Xamoschi in Japan. He showed the custom officer his letter from the emperor of Luggnagg to his imperial majesty, the emperor of Japan. They knew the real very well, it was as broad as the palm of his hand.

The magistrate received him as a public minister. They provided him carriage and servants and carried to Yedo, the metropolitan city, where he was admitted to an audience and his letter was opened with great ceremony and explained to the emperor by an interpreter. Gulliver presented himself as a Dutch merchant who wanted to return of his country.

So, he asked the emperor's royal favour to give order to take him to Nangasac. He also wished to be exempted from the caremony of trampling upon the crucifix. The emperor was surprised at this offer and gathered him the permission to do so. And granted him the permission to do so. But he said that the crucifix episode should pass off as mere forgetfulness, otherwise his countrymen would not leave him alive.

Gulliver thanked him. He was sent to Nangasac with some troops marching to that place with instructions to the commanding officer to make him reach there safely.

Part IV 1

Introduction

Gulliver sets on his fourth voyage as a captain of a ship. Then he follows his encounter with the hairy monsters and finally with Houyhnhnms.

Gulliver is Marooned Ashore

Gulliver returns from his third voyage and spends about five months at home with his family in England. Gulliver sets on his fourth voyage leaving his wife pregnant.

He sets sail on the ship called the Adventurer, this time as a captain. He takes an expert Robert Purefoy with him. Many of his sailors die of a fever of tropical climates, so he hires some new recruits from Barbados. His crew members mutiny under the influence of the new sailors and become pirates. They captivate Gulliver in his own cabin. In May, 1711, Gulliver is left alone on an inhibited island.

Gulliver's Encounter with the Hairy Monsters

They appear like naked, monsters with long hair and sharp claws which they use for climbing trees. Gulliver is depressed at their hateful sight. He decides to search for settlers in this land. While searching he encounters one of the animal. Gulliver hits it with the flat side of his sword.

The animal roars loudly and a herd of about forty other hairy monsters attacks Gulliver. Gulliver seeks shelter in a tree, shaking his sword to scare the animals back, but they try to avenge him by defeating him.

1

परिचय

Gulliver (गुलिवर) जहाज के कप्तान के रूप में अपनी चौथी यात्रा का शुभारंभ करता है। इसके पश्चात् उसका सामना लंबे बालों वाले दैत्यों से होता है तथा अंततः उसका सामना Houyhnhnms (हायोम्स) से भी होता है।

गुलिवर का किनारे पर असहाय होना

गुलिवर अपनी तीसरी समुद्री यात्रा से लौटकर आता है तथा लगभग पाँच महीनों का वक्त इंग्लैंड में अपने परिवार के साथ बिताता है। गुलिवर अपनी गर्भवती पत्नी को छोड़कर चौथी समुद्री यात्रा पर निकल पड़ता है।

वह एक जहाज जिसे Adventure (एडवेंचरर) के नाम से जाना जाता है को अपनी यात्रा हेतु उपयुक्त मानकर उस जहाज के कप्तान के तौर पर अपनी यात्रा की शुरूआत करता है। वह अपने साथ Robert Purefoy (रॉबर्ट प्योरफॉय) नामक एक निपुण व्यक्ति को ले जाता है। Tropical (उष्णकटिबंधीय) जलवायु के एक बुखार से उसके कई साथी नाविकों की मृत्यु हो जाती है जिस कारण वह Barbados (बारबडोस) प्रांत से कुछ नए नाविकों की नियुक्ति करता है। उसके साथी सदस्य नए नाविकों के बहकावे में आ जाते हैं तथा बगावत कर देते हैं। वे सभी गुलिवर को उसके ही कक्ष में बंधक बना लेते हैं। मई, 1711 में गुलिवर को एक निर्जन द्वीप पर छोड़ दिया जाता है।

गुलिवर का सामना बालों वाले दैत्यों से होना

वे लोग नग्न, लंबे बालों वाले दैत्य प्रतीत होते हैं तथा उनके पंजे काफी तीक्ष्ण हैं, जिनका प्रयोग वे वृक्षों पर चढ़ने हेतु करते हैं। गुलिवर को उनकी घृणास्पद दशा को देखकर आश्चर्यपूर्ण निराशा होती है। वह इस भूमि पर रहने वालों की खोज करने का निर्णय लेता है। ढूँढते हुए वह एक जानवर के सामने आ जाता है। गुलिवर इस पर अपनी तलवार की धार से प्रहार करता है।

वह जानवर ऊँची आवाज में चिंघाड़ता है तथा लगभग चालीस दैत्याकार जानवरों का एक समूह गुलिवर पर हमला कर देता है। गुलिवर एक वृक्ष का सहारा लेकर अपनी जान बचाता है तथा वह जानवरों को डराने के लिए अपनी तलवार को लहराता है, परंतु वे उसे हराकर उससे बदला लेने की कोशिश करते हैं।

Word Meaning

Foundered	– पानी से भरा एवं डूबा हुआ	Recruits	– समूह के नए सदस्य
Buccaneer	– समुद्री डाकू	Plunder	– लूटपाट करना
Expostulated	– तर्क किया	Desolate	– सुनसान
Lank	– निस्तेज	Antipathy	– द्वेष
Visage	– चेहरा	Maimed	– घायल
Persecutor	– उत्पीड़क	Odious	– अप्रिय
Disdain	– अवहेलना	Articulate	– साफ बोलना
Orthography	– वर्तनी	Metamorphosed	– बदला हुआ
Conjurer	– जादूगर	Discomposed	– व्यथित

Important Questions

Questions based on the Plot of the Chapter

Q 1. What problems did Gulliver face while sailing?

गुलिवर को नौकायन के दौरान किन-किन समस्याओं का सामना करना पड़ा?

गुलिवर का उत्साही व्यक्ति होना तथा समुद्र के रहस्यों को उजागर करने हेतु लालायित होना– तीसरी समुद्री यात्रा से लौटकर चौथी यात्रा पर जाने का निर्णय लेना – इस यात्रा के दौरान तमाम मुश्किलें आना – एडवेंचरर नामक जहाज पर कप्तान के रूप में शुरूआत करना – निपुण रॉबर्ट प्योरफॉय का गुलिवर के साथ होना, परंतु कई नाविकों का बुखार की वजह से मृत होना – गुलिवर द्वारा नए नाविकों की भर्ती करना – नए नाविकों का पुराने नाविकों के साथ बगावत करना – गुलिवर को बंधक बनाया जाना तथा एक निर्जन द्वीप पर छोड़ दिया जाना।

Ans. Gulliver was an adventurous person and he wanted to explore the secrets of sea and islands. After returning from his third voyage, he decided to set out for the next one. After passing some time with his family, he left for his next voyage without any anxiety. He was a zealous person and he never cared for possible problems, but this time he had to face various difficulties.

He took a ship named 'Adventurer' for sailing and he started his journey as the captain of that ship. An expert Robert Purefoy was with him, but most of his fellow sailors died because of a mysterious fever of tropical climate and this was a big issue for him.

In order to make a new crew, he had to recruit some new sailors. This proved a curse for him later because the newly recruited sailors instigated the old ones and they collectively rebelled against Gulliver. Gulliver was captivated and marooned ashore later. Thus, Gulliver had to face various problems during his journey.

Q 2. Describe Gulliver's encounter with the hairy beasts.

बालों वाले दैत्यों से गुलिवर का सामना कैसे हुआ? वर्णन करिए।

गुलिवर का अपने साथियों के आकस्मिक व्यवहार से आहत होना – गुलिवर के साथियों का विद्रोह करना तथा उसे निर्जन द्वीप पर छोड़ देना – गुलिवर का वहाँ व्यक्तियों की तलाश करना – गुलिवर का विचित्र प्राणियों को देखकर अचंभित होना, क्योंकि उन प्राणियों का नग्न अवस्था में होना तथा शारीरिक विंयास असामान्य होना – गुलिवर का उनसे बचने का प्रयास करना, परंतु एक प्राणी से उसका सामना हो जाना – गुलिवर का उस पर प्रहार करना तथा भड़के हुए प्राणियों के झुंड का गुलिवर पर पुनः हमला करना– गुलिवर का खुद को बचाने का प्रयत्न करना, परंतु पूर्ण रूप से सफल न होना – एक घोड़े का आना एवं प्राणियों का डरकर भाग जाना।

Ans. Gulliver was very troubled because of the unexpected behaviours of his crewmen towards him. They rebelled against him and finally they left him on an inhibited island. Gulliver decided to explore that new island and in order to do this, he started searching people there. He could not find any person there, but he found some strange creatures in a large number.

Those creatures were in naked state and looking like monsters with their long hair and different style of beard. Gulliver became much surprised after seeing them because they had very sharp claws, which they were using in climbing trees.

Gulliver did not want to face them, but suddenly a creature appeared before him. Gulliver hit that creature with his sword which made the herd much agitated and they collectively attacked on him.

Gulliver continued his efforts of saving himself, but those creatures were very rigid and they wanted to harm him at any cost. Finally, entry of a horse changed the scenario and saved Gulliver from those strange creatures.

Introduction

The gray horse leads Gulliver to his house. Gulliver comes across the Yahoos who appear as disgusting creatures, tied to a wall with a rope and devouring offensive food. The horses are well-mannered, modest and decent, while the Yahoos are ugly, evoking hatred and frustration.

Gulliver is Led to the House of Horses

The gray horse leads Gulliver to a long, low building. Gulliver takes out gifts to distribute among the hosts. But he finds that there are many horses in the house doing various activities. He thinks that the house belong to a very important person.

He wonders why so many horses are employed for servants. Gulliver arrives at a house where he comes across a horse who utters the word 'Yahoo'.

Gulliver Meets 'Yahoos'

Gulliver is taken to the courtyard, where some of the detestable hairy creatures are tied up with a rope to a wall. The horse leader orders a horse to unchain one of the creatures and bring him before Gulliver. To his shock and dismay, Gulliver discovers the creature resembles the human being. Now Gulliver learns that the Yahoo signifies a human being. His hands have uncut nails and he is a bit hair and more callous than Gulliver, but still, he is undoubtedly a human being.

Word Meaning

Building	– भवन	Kindly	– भली-भाँति
Opinion	– विचार	Dialect	– भाषा
Necromancy	– काला जादू	Contemptuous	– घृणित
Creatures	– प्राणी	Abominable	– डरावना

परिचय

Gray horse (ग्रे घोड़ा) गुलिवर को घर तक लेकर जाता है। वहाँ पहुँचकर Gulliver (गुलिवर) Yahoo (याहू) प्राणियों को देखता है, जो अत्यंत घृणित प्रतीत हो रहे हैं तथा एक दीवार से रस्सी द्वारा बँधे हुए हैं और अभद्र रूप से भोजन कर रहे हैं। घोड़े अत्यंत सभ्य, अच्छे आचरण वाले तथा प्रसन्नता प्रदान करने वाले हैं, जबकि याहू प्राणी अत्यंत भद्दे, अरुचिकर तथा अशिष्ट हैं।

गुलिवर का घोड़ों के घर पहुँच जाना

ग्रे घोड़ा गुलिवर को लंबे तथा अपेक्षाकृत कम ऊँचाई वाले भवन की ओर लेकर जाता है। गुलिवर मेजबानों को देने हेतु उपहार निकालता है, परंतु वह पाता है कि वहाँ अत्यधिक घोड़े हैं और सभी घर में अलग-अलग कार्य कर रहे हैं। वह सोचता है कि घर किसी महत्त्वशाली व्यक्ति का होगा।

उसे आश्चर्य है कि नौकरों के स्थान पर इतने ज्यादा घोड़े क्यों लगाए गए हैं। जहाँ वह एक घोड़े को देखता है, जो 'याहू' शब्द बोलता है।

गुलिवर की मुलाकात 'याहू' से हुई

गुलिवर को आगे एक आँगननुमा स्थान मिलता है, जहाँ वह देखता है कि कुछ भद्दे बालों वाले दैत्याकार प्राणी एक दीवार से रस्सी से बँधे हुए हैं। घोड़ों का मुखिया एक घोड़े को आदेश देता है कि एक बालों वाले दैत्याकार को मुक्त करके गुलिवर के समक्ष प्रस्तुत करे। गुलिवर को तब अत्यंत विस्मय होता है जब वह देखता है कि वह प्राणी मनुष्य जैसा लग रहा है। तब गुलिवर को अनुभव हो जाता है कि 'याहू' शब्द मनुष्य हेतु प्रयुक्त होता है। उस प्राणी के नाखून बढ़े हुए हैं तथा बाल भी लंबे हो गए हैं, वह थोड़ा विचित्र लग रहा है, परंतु वह एक मनुष्य ही है।

Coarseness	– खुरदरापन	Steed	– परिपक्व घोड़ा
Insipid	– बेस्वाद	Sufficient	– पर्याप्त
Winnow	– अलग करना	Sustenance	– भोजन

Important Questions

Questions based on the Plot of the Chapter

Q 1. Where did the gray horse lead Gulliver to? What did he see there? How was Gulliver received?

ग्रे घोड़ा गुलिवर को कहाँ लेकर गया? उसने वहाँ क्या देखा? गुलिवर के साथ वहाँ कैसा बर्ताव हुआ?

गुलिवर के पास कोई विकल्प न होना – उसे भोजन एवं शरण की आस होना – उसका घोड़ों का अनुसरण करना – घोड़ों द्वारा उसे एक विचित्र घर में लाया जाना – वहाँ गुलिवर द्वारा याहू प्राणियों को देखना – गुलिवर का परेशान हो जाना क्योंकि याहू प्राणियों का अत्यंत घृणित होना – गुलिवर द्वारा घोड़ों एवं याहू प्राणियों में कई अंतर पाना – घोड़ों द्वारा गुलिवर का स्वागत बेहतर तरीके से किया जाना – घोड़ों द्वारा उसे पीने हेतु दूध दिया जाना – किसी प्राणी द्वारा गुलिवर को कोई नुकसान न पहुँचाया जाना।

Ans. Gulliver had not any other option, so he decided to follow both horses because he wanted some food, shelter and other better aspects. The horses lead Gulliver to a house which was quite strange for Gulliver in many ways. When Gulliver entered the house, he saw there Yahoo creatures who were appearing very hateful for Gulliver. He saw there that those Yahoo creatures were tied to a wall with a rope and they were devouring food. Gulliver was very confused and he wanted to get rid of that horrible sight. He found a lot of differences between the horses and those Yahoo creatures because the horses were well-mannered and modest whereas the Yahoo creatures were quite offensive and ugly. However, Gulliver got well reception there and the horses welcomed him very much. He was given a large quantity of milk, with the help of which he became successful in satisfying his hunger. In addition to this, no creature tried to harm Gulliver, which was a satisfactory thing for him.

Q 2. Describe the behaviour of the horses towards Gulliver.

घोड़ों के गुलिवर के प्रति व्यवहार का वर्णन करिए।

घोड़ों का गुलिवर को अपने निवास स्थान पर देखकर विचित्र व्यवहार करना – उनका गुलिवर के प्रति उदार होना – उनका गुलिवर के विषय में संशयपूर्ण भी होना – उनके द्वारा गुलिवर हेतु कई प्रकार के परीक्षण कराए जाना – घोड़ों द्वारा गुलिवर को उनकी

भाषा के शब्द बताने का इच्छुक होना – घोड़ों द्वारा गुलिवर के कम खाने को लेकर चिंतित होना – प्रारंभिक अवस्था में गुलिवर का हिचकिचाना, परंतु बाद में उसके द्वारा घोड़ों का साथ पसंद किया जाना – घोड़ों द्वारा उसे पीने के लिए दूध एवं सोने हेतु स्थान दिया जाना – गुलिवर का प्रसन्न हो जाना।

Ans. The horses behaved in a different manner when they found Gulliver in their living place. They were humble towards him, but they were doubtful regarding him also. They were unable to determine the category of Gulliver and this was a disturbing issue for him because he had to face various observatory tests in order to get their doubt cleared. However, all the horses were quite humble and non offensive towards him and they were very eager to teach him the pronunciation of the words in their language. They were much concerned about Gulliver because according to them, the diet of Gulliver was too low. Gulliver was also very hesitated in initial phase because he was unable to understand them, but later he began to enjoy the company of those horses as they provided him a lot of milk to drink and a space to sleep which was urgent requirement of Gulliver. Thus, Gulliver felt a lot of comfort in the company of those horses as all the horses were quite humble towards him.

Question based on the Character Sketch

Q 3. On the basis of this chapter, give a brief character sketch of horses.

अध्याय के आधार पर घोड़ों का संक्षिप्त चरित्र चित्रण करिए।

घोड़ों का सभ्य एवं उदार होना – उनके द्वारा गुलिवर से अच्छा व्यवहार किया जाना – उनके द्वारा गुलिवर को भोजन एवं शरण देना – घोड़ों का गुलिवर के विषय में संदेह युक्त होना – घोड़ों का गुलिवर को 'याहू' समझना – उनके द्वारा परीक्षण किया जाना – गुलिवर का 'याहू' न होना घोड़ों का ध्यान देने वाले जानवर होना – उनके द्वारा गुलिवर को भोजन एवं शरण उपलब्ध कराया गया।

Ans. The horses were well-mannered and modest because they did not make any attempt to harm Gulliver. They were very co-operative for Gulliver as they provided food and shelter to him.

On the basis of this chapter, we see following traits in their characteristics

Doubtful The horses were initially doubtful towards Gulliver because they were not sure about the category of Gulliver. They took him as a Yahoo and actually Gulliver was not a Yahoo. However, they conducted various tests and later they came to know that Gulliver was different from Yahoo creatures.

Gulliver Learns the Language of Houyhnhnms

Gulliver tries to learn the languages of the horses. He can now talk with the Houyhnhnms. Gulliver is visited by many Houyhnhnms who are wonderstruck to see that Gulliver possesses reason. After three months, Gulliver is able to answer most of the questions asked by the master horse. Gulliver reveals to him that he arrived at his island in a ship. His ship was made and even sailed by men.

गुलिवर का हायोम्स की भाषा सीख लेना

Gulliver (गुलिवर) घोड़ों की भाषा सीखने की कोशिश करता है। अब वह Houyhnhnms (हायोम्स) से बातचीत कर सकता है। गुलिवर से मिलने बहुत से हायोम्स आते हैं, जिन्हें गुलिवर की अद्‌भुत तर्कशक्ति पर अचरज होता है। तीन महीनों के प्रयत्न के पश्चात् गुलिवर घोड़ों के स्वामी के सवालों का जवाब देने में सक्षम हो जाता है। गुलिवर उसे बताता है कि वह उसके द्वीप पर एक जहाज द्वारा आया है। उसका जहाज मनुष्यों द्वारा बनाया हुआ था तथा मनुष्य ही उसे चलाते थे।

The Naked Truth

Gulliver is reluctant to disclose the fact that he really is like the other Yahoos, but in vain. But the sorrel nag is influenced even by Gulliver's naked body as Gulliver is very different from the other Yahoos, since he has a pale, soft and relatively hairless skin. Gulliver forbids the master horse to call him a Yahoo and not to disclose the secret of his being Yahoo. The master horse agrees.

एक सत्य

गुलिवर अनिच्छा से व्यक्त करता है कि वह वास्तव में अन्य Yahoos (याहू) प्राणियों की तरह है, परंतु सब व्यर्थ रहता है। वह घोड़ा गुदिलवर के नग्न शरीर को देखकर प्रभावित होता है, क्योंकि गुलिवर का शरीर अन्य याहू प्राणियों से भिन्न है, क्योंकि उसकी त्वचा हल्की पीली, अपेक्षाकृत मुलायम थी तथा उसकी त्वचा पर बाल नहीं थे। गुलिवर घोड़ों के स्वामी को मना करता है कि वह उसे याहू संबोधित न करे और उसके याहू होने की बात को उजागर न करे। घोड़ों का स्वामी निवेदन स्वीकार कर लेता है।

Word Meaning

Desirous	– इच्छुक	Brute	– क्रूर
Significant	– महत्त्वपूर्ण	Proficiency	– दक्षता
Disposition	– प्रकृति	Progress	– प्रगति
Valet	– पुरुष दास	Conceal	– छिपाना
Performance	– प्रदर्शन	Affectation	– दिखावा
Odious	– घृणित	Tedious	– थकाने वाला
Persecution	– बुरा बर्ताव	Degenerate	– समाप्त होना

Important Questions

Questions based on the Plot of the Chapter

Q 1. What questions were asked by the master horse and how did Gulliver satisfy him?

घोड़ों के स्वामी ने क्या प्रश्न पूछे एवं गुलिवर ने उसे किस प्रकार संतुष्ट किया?

गुलिवर का बेहतर प्रकार से प्रयत्न करके घोड़ों की भाषा समझने के लायक हो जाना – घोड़ों के स्वामी का गुलिवर के निवास के विषय में पूछना तथा उस द्वीप तक पहुँचने के विषय में पूछना – गुलिवर का उसे बताना कि वह जहाज में आया है, जिसका वह स्वयं कप्तान है – गुलिवर का वापस जाने की उत्सुकता भी व्यक्त करना – घोड़ों के स्वामी का गुलिवर से बात करके उसे भली-भाँति जान लेना।

Ans. Gulliver tried his best and soon he became able to learn the language of horses. The master horse asked various questions to Gulliver and Gulliver answered all questions and told almost everything about himself.

The master horse asked him from where he had come and how he had reached here, on which Gulliver told him about his arrival. Gulliver told him that he came there in a ship and he himself was the leader of his ship.

Gulliver expressed his concern about his returning because he wanted to tell the Englishmen about different tradition of that island. The master horse was satisfied after talking to Gulliver because he answered everything asked by the master horse which helped the horses in understanding Gulliver completely.

Gulliver Reveals the Truth of England

Gulliver converses with the master horse and informs about the treatment of the Yahoos and horses in England. He does not disapprove of what Gulliver tells him. Gulliver explains to the master horse how he sailed in a boat made by men and how the Yahoos are served in England by the horses. The master horse suspects if Gulliver is telling a lie, but the horses are not aware of the concept of mischief or lying. The master horse is totally depressed to learn that the horses in England are used for travelling, riding, drawing chariots and racing.

गुलिवर का इंग्लैंड से जुड़े सत्य को उजागर करना

गुलिवर घोड़ों के स्वामी से बातें करने लगता है और उसे बताता है कि याहू प्राणी एवं घोड़े इंग्लैंड में किस प्रकार का व्यवहार करते हैं। घोड़ों का स्वामी गुलिवर द्वारा दी गई सूचनाओं को अस्वीकार नहीं करता। गुलिवर घोड़ों के स्वामी को बताता है कि वह किस प्रकार मनुष्यों द्वारा निर्मित एक जहाज में आया था तथा किस प्रकार घोड़े इंग्लैंड में याहू प्राणियों की सेवा करते हैं। घोड़ों के स्वामी को गुलिवर के झूठ बोलने की शंका भी होती है, परंतु घोड़े झूठ बोलने अथवा शरारत की अवधारणाओं से अपरिचित होते हैं। घोड़ों के स्वामी को यह जानकर अत्यंत निराशा होती है कि इंग्लैंड में घोड़ों का इस्तेमाल यात्रा करने, घुड़सवारी करने, रथ खींचने तथा दौड़ प्रतियोगिताओं में होता है।

Word Meaning

Countenance – समर्थन करना
Conception – विचार
Drudgery – कठिन परिश्रम
Resentment – क्रोध, नाराजगी
Strangers – अजनबी
Intemperance – लालच
Particular – विशेष रूप से
Digression – विषय से भटकाव
Tractable – सुविधाजनक
Venture – उपक्रम
Antipathy – विरोध
Perjury – झूठी गवाही
Insuperable – अजेय
Improved – बेहतर

Important Questions

Questions based on the Plot of the Chapter

Q 1. What was the reaction of the master horse to Gulliver's narrative?

गुलिवर की बातों को सुनकर घोड़ों के स्वामी ने क्या प्रतिक्रिया दी?

गुलिवर का घोड़ों के लिए आश्चर्यपूर्ण होना – घोड़ों के स्वामी का अनुभवी होना तथा गुलिवर का सहयोग करना – गुलिवर का उसे अपने विषय में सब कुछ बताना – प्रारंभ में घोड़ों के स्वामी का गुलिवर पर संशय करना, परंतु बाद में उसे गुलिवर पर पूरा भरोसा हो जाना – गुलिवर का अपने देश एवं सभ्यता के विषय में बहुत कुछ बताना – घोड़ों के स्वामी तथा अन्य गुलाम घोड़ों का गुलिवर को ध्यानपूर्वक सुनना – घोड़ों के स्वामी का घोड़ों की दुर्दशा पर चिंता एवं बाद में क्रोध व्यक्त करना – घोड़ों के स्वामी का घोड़ों की महत्ता का सम्मान करना।

Ans. Gulliver was a surprise for all those horses because he was an alien for those horses. The master horse was veteran, mature and co-operative with Gulliver. Gulliver told the story of all incidents happened with him in process of reaching that island. However, the master horse was initially doubtful about the story of Gulliver, but later the situation changed.

The master horse started to believe Gulliver. Gulliver explained various issues of his culture, his country and so on which was quite interesting for the master horse. The master horse kept control over other horses, so other horses were bound to follow the master horse.

Everyting was well during the conversation of Gulliver and the master horse except a concern of the master horse regarding the pitiable situation of horses in England which later leads the master horse towards an extreme anger.

The master horse could not accept the domination of any species over horses. Gulliver became surprised on the reaction of the master horse, but he continued telling truth to the master horse.

Introduction

Gulliver explains to the master horse the recent English history, the reasons of war and how law is abused in society of humans, leaving the master horse depressed.

Causes of the War

Gulliver informs the master horse about the Glorious Revolution in 1689 under the Prince of Orange and the long war of the Spanish Succession from 1701 to 1714. The master horse wants to know the causes of war in Gulliver's society. Gulliver answers that causes of war include lack of land or people to govern, differences of opinion, ambition to conquer, etc.

According to the master horse, the Yahoos are formed by the nature in such a way that they cannot harm one another nor are their mouths and claws fit for fighting.

Law Defined

Law, according to the master horse, is meant to sustain life, not destroy it. Then Gulliver explains how law is abused in human society. A lawyer is a disguised liar in reality for, he is paid to argue that white is black and black is white. He defends falsehood and not justice. The language of the lawyers can be understood by none.

Word Meaning

Satisfaction – संतोष
Clamour – कोलाहल
Ally – मित्र
Strewed – बिखरा हुआ
Barbarous – असभ्य
Vice – दुर्गुण
Variance – भिन्नता
Distorted – अस्पष्ट

5

परिचय

Gulliver (गुलिवर) घोड़ों के स्वामी को England (इंग्लैंड) के हालिया History (इतिहास) के बारे में सब कुछ बताता है तथा उसे युद्ध के कारण और कैसे नियम-कानूनों का मानव समाज में अपमान किया जाता है, भी बताता है, यह सब सुनकर घोड़ों के स्वामी को अत्यंत दु:ख होता है।

युद्ध के कारण

गुलिवर घोड़ों के स्वामी को Orange (ऑरेंज) शासक के नेतृत्व में 1689 में हुई गौरवशाली क्रांति के बारे में बताता है तथा Spanish (स्पेन) में उत्तराधिकार हेतु 1701 से 1714 तक चले War (युद्ध) की भी पूरी कहानी बताता है। घोड़ों का स्वामी गुलिवर के समाज में होने वाले युद्ध के कारण जानना चाहता है। गुलिवर उसे युद्ध के अनेक कारण बताता है; जैसे– भूमि की कमी, लोगों की शासक बनने की इच्छा, वैचारिक मतभेद, विजय की लालसा आदि।

घोड़ों के स्वामी के अनुसार, याहू प्राणियों की प्राकृतिक संरचना ही ऐसी होती है कि वे एक-दूसरे को नुकसान नहीं पहुँचा सकते तथा उनके मुख और पंजे कुछ भी युद्ध हेतु उपयुक्त नहीं होते।

नियमों की व्याख्या

घोड़ों के स्वामी के अनुसार नियम-कानून जीवन को आसान बनाने के लिए होते हैं ना कि उसे तबाह करने हेतु। तब गुलिवर उसे बताता है कि किस प्रकार मानव समाज में नियम कानूनों के साथ खिलवाड़ होता है। अधिवक्ता एक नकाबपोश झूठ बोलने वाला व्यक्ति होता है जिसे सच को झूठ एवं झूठ को सच साबित करने के पैसे दिए जाते हैं। वह सदैव झूठों का बचाव करता है तथा वह किसी भी प्रकार से न्याय नहीं करता है। अधिवक्ताओं की भाषा किसी को भी समझ नहीं आती।

Vile – घृणित
Injustice – अन्याय
Adversary – शत्रु
Iniquitous – दुष्टतापूर्ण
Plundering – लूटना
Preserve – सुरक्षित करना
Dextrous – कुशल

Important Questions

Questions based on the Plot of the Chapter

Q 1. What did Gulliver inform the master horse about the recent history of England?

गुलिवर ने घोड़ों के स्वामी को इंग्लैंड के हालिया इतिहास के विषय में क्या बताया?

घोड़ों के स्वामी का गुलिवर से सवाल पूछना – गुलिवर का उन सवालों के जवाब देना – घोड़ों के स्वामी का इंग्लैंड के विषय में सब कुछ जानने की इच्छा व्यक्त करना – गुलिवर का उसे इंग्लैंड का हालिया इतिहास बताना – गुलिवर का घोड़ों के स्वामी को ऑरेंज के शासक के नेतृत्व में हुई महान् क्रांति के विषय में बताना – गुलिवर का घोड़ों के स्वामी को बताना कि किस प्रकार युद्ध के दौरान निर्दोष लोगों की जानें जाती हैं तथा कानूनों की अवहेलना की जाती है।

Ans. The master horse asked various questions to Gulliver and Gulliver answered all of them. The master horse was interested in knowing everything related to English culture and history of England and Gulliver fulfilled the wish of the master horse. Gulliver explained various issues of history of England and he told the master horse about the great revolution under the Prince of Orange, the long war with the France, the story of succession, the queen and so on. Gulliver further told the master horse about the horrible aspects of the war, he explained how law was abused during war and how a number of persons was pilled unreasonally. This all was quite disturbing for the master horse and the master horse became sad. Further the master horse asked about the causes and consequences of war because for the society of those horses, war was nothing but a totally new concept.

Q 2. What were the causes of war explained by Gulliver?

गुलिवर के द्वारा बताए हुए युद्ध के कारण क्या-क्या थे?

इंग्लैंड का इतिहास जानने हेतु घोड़ों के स्वामी का गुलिवर से कई बातें पूछना – गुलिवर का घोड़ों के स्वामी को इंग्लैंड के इतिहास के विषय में बताना तथा युद्ध की विभीषिका का भी जिक्र करना – घोड़ों के स्वामी का परेशान हो जाना तथा गुलिवर से युद्ध के कारणों के विषय में पूछना – गुलिवर का घोड़ों के स्वामी को बताना कि भूमि की कमी, लोगों द्वारा शासन की इच्छा, वैचारिक मतभेद, जीतने की लालसा आदि ही युद्ध के मुख्य कारण थे

Ans. The master horse asked various questions to Gulliver because it was an interesting thing for the master horse to know about the history of England. Gulliver told various issues to the master horse including the story of war which made the master horse almost speechless. Gulliver further explained the horrific scenario of war then the master horse asked Gulliver what were the reasons of war in England? Gulliver knew that there was a number of reasons of war, but he decided to explain some of the prominent ones. Gulliver told the master horse that there were various causes of war like issues of lack of land, wish of people to govern, differences of opinion, ambition to conquer and so on. Gulliver told that a nation could be invaded only after occurence of famine or civil unrest in his society and that's why usually wars occured in order to create civil unrest. Gulliver was also against of wars and all types of bad practices.

Q 3. What were laws in human society? How were they abused and by whom? Explain in Gulliver's words.

मानव समाज में कानून क्या थे? इनका किस प्रकार एवं किसके द्वारा उल्लंघन किया जाता था? गुलिवर के शब्दों में व्यक्त करिए।

घोड़ों के स्वामी ने बताया कि कानून जीवन को सरल बनाने हेतु होते हैं ना कि जीवन नष्ट करने हेतु – गुलिवर का मानव समाज में कानून के व्यंग्यपूर्ण चित्रण को प्रस्तुत करना – उसका अपनी बात साबित करने हेतु वकीलों का उदाहरण देना – उसका बताना कि वकील पेशेवर झूठ बोलने वाले व्यक्ति होते हैं, जिन्हें भ्रष्ट रूप से तर्क करने हेतु धन दिया जाता है – न्याय देने में देरी, झूठे मामले बनाना आदि गतिविधियों द्वारा वकीलों का लाभ कमाना – घोड़ों के स्वामी का इस दुःखद पहलू को जानकर निराश होना।

Ans. The master horse explained that law is meant to sustain life, not to destroy it, but Gulliver contradicted the perception of the master horse by giving the satirical picture of law in human society. Gulliver explained that in human society, law is abused. However, Gulliver tried to prove his statement and for this, he provided the example of lawyers. According to him, lawyers were none but professional liars who were paid for false arguments and they were morally degraded. Gulliver further told the master horse that the language of lawyers was quite incomprehensible for everyone because they did everything in their profession just for their own benefits and not for real justice.

Delaying in decisions, making false cases and so on were some other examples of bad practices of lawyers. The master horse became very disturbed because according to the master horse, it was just wastage of money to train such type of lawyers.

6

Greedy Lawyers

It is difficult for the master horse to understand what could inspire lawyers to injure their fellow humans. Gulliver explains that it is the greed or desire for money which instigates the lawyers to torment their fellow humans. But the concept of money is totally missing in the land of the Houyhnhnms.

The Rich

Money is so powerful that it enables a Yahoo to do anything he wants to. He can purchase the best properties, dresses and provisions and above all, the most beautiful woman.

A Yahoo is never satisfied with the amount of money he is having as he wants to have more and more of it. The ratio of the rich and the poor is quite unproportionate as for every rich man, there are a thousand poor. Besides, the rich live off the drudgery of the poor.

Politics

Now Gulliver diverts to politics. He lists the characteristic requisites for a Chief Minister in the government, the most significant being hypocrisy.

If the candidate publicly defames the court, he will be choosen as Chief Minister because such overenthusiastic people always prove flattering and submissive. He preserves his chair by bribing Members of Parliament.

Word Meaning

Confederacy – संधि
Hectoring – धमकी भरा
Nauseous – घृणाजनक
Precious – संपत्ति
Imaginations – कल्पनाएँ
Contrive – युक्ति निकालना

लोभी वकील

घोड़ों के स्वामी हेतु यह समझना जटिल है कि ऐसे कौन-से कारण हैं, जो वकीलों को अपने साथी मनुष्यों से छल करने हेतु प्रेरित करते हैं। गुलिवर उसे बताता है कि लोभ एवं धन की लालसा वकीलों को अपने साथी मनुष्यों का शोषण करने के लिए उत्तेजित करती हैं। परंतु Houyhnhnms (हायोम्स) की दुनिया में धन की अवधारणा है ही नहीं।

धनी लोग

Money (धन) में इतनी शक्ति होती है कि एक याहू प्राणी इससे किसी भी वस्तु को खरीद सकता है। मनुष्य इससे बेहतरीन Properties (संपत्तियाँ), वस्त्र, विभिन्न वस्तुएँ और इन सबसे भी अधिक महत्त्वपूर्ण खूबसूरत महिला को हासिल कर सकता है।

एक याहू प्राणी कभी भी अपने धन की मात्रा से संतुष्ट नहीं होता क्योंकि उसमें सदैव अधिक धन पाने की लालसा बनी रहती है। धनी व्यक्तियों एवं निर्धन व्यक्तियों के मध्य अनुपात अत्यंत असमान है क्योंकि एक धनी व्यक्ति के सापेक्ष हजारों निर्धन व्यक्ति हैं। इसके अतिरिक्त, धनी व्यक्ति निर्धन व्यक्तियों का शोषण करते हैं।

राजनीति

इसके पश्चात् गुलिवर Politics (राजनीति) के विषय पर वार्ता प्रारंभ कर देता है। वह बताता है कि राज्य का Chief Minister (मुख्यमंत्री) बनने हेतु कौन-कौन से गुण आवश्यक होते हैं तथा वह यह भी बताता है कि सबसे जरूरी गुण है मिथ्या चरित्र होना।

यदि उम्मीदवार सार्वजनिक रूप से न्यायालय की अवहेलना करे, तो उसे अवश्य मुख्यमंत्री चुन लिया जायेगा, क्योंकि ऐसे लोग सदैव चापलूस एवं विनम्र साबित होते हैं। मुख्यमंत्री चुने जाने के पश्चात् ऐसे लोग अपनी पदवी बचाए रखने हेतु Members of Parliament (संसद सदस्यों) को रिश्वत देते रहते हैं।

Malady – बीमारी
Sagacity – बुद्धिमत्ता
Lackey – नौकर
Portending – पूर्वाभास
Forlorn – दु:खी
Rudiment – प्राथमिक ज्ञान

Important Questions

Questions based on the Plot of the Chapter

Q 1. Describe Gulliver's explanation regarding money and the rich.

गुलिवर की धन एवं धनी लोगों की व्याख्या का वर्णन करें।

गुलिवर एवं घोड़ों के स्वामी का बातों में व्यस्त होना – गुलिवर का घोड़ों के स्वामी को कई बातें बताना – अधिकांश बातें घोड़ों की दुनिया हेतु नवीन होने के कारण घोड़ों के स्वामी का उन्हें ना समझ पाना – गुलिवर का घोड़ों के स्वामी को धन की महत्ता के विषय में बताना – गुलिवर का उसे बताना कि धनी व्यक्ति जो चाहे हासिल कर सकता है; जैसे– संपत्ति, बहुमूल्य वस्तुएँ, खूबसूरत महिला आदि– गुलिवर का घोड़ों के स्वामी को धनी लोगों की दिखावापूर्ण जीवन शैली के विषय में बताना – उसका यह भी बताना कि धन अत्यधिक अभिमान एवं चिंता का कारक है– उसके बावजूद व्यक्तियों का धनार्जन में व्यस्त रहना।

Ans. Gulliver and the master horse were involved in a discussion and Gulliver presented the actual view of various issues in front of the master horse.

The master horse could not understand a major portion of Gulliver's aspects because things which were being mentioned by Gulliver were quite new for the world of horses. Gulliver told the master horse that money is the most important matter in human society because a person having money gets the right to enjoy everything automatically.

Gulliver further explained that if a person is wealthy, all the amenities are accessible to him like property, precious possession, beautiful woman, etc. Gulliver presented the picture of extravagance being practised by so called wealthy persons. He explained that a person who becomes wealthy, starts to forget how to behave passionately with others.

Money, wealth and all other assets bring a lot of proud, a lot of anxieties to the holder, but in the human society, everyone is involved in collecting more and more wealth.

Q 2. What did Gulliver tell the master horse about politics as it existed in England?

गुलिवर ने घोड़ों के स्वामी को इंग्लैंड की राजनीति के विषय में क्या बताया?

गुलिवर का घोड़ों के स्वामी को इंग्लैंड की राजनीति के विषय में बताना – घोड़ों के स्वामी का सच जानकर परेशान हो जाना – गुलिवर का राजनीतिज्ञों के लिए आवश्यक गुणों के विषय में बताना – गुलिवर का उसे बताना कि न्यायालय की अवहेलना करने वाले व्यक्ति का मुख्यमंत्री चुन लिया जाना तथा उस व्यक्ति का चापलूसी से परिपूर्ण होना – ऐसे व्यक्ति का लक्ष्य मात्र अपना स्थान सुरक्षित किए रहना होना – ऐसे व्यक्ति का जनता के प्रति जवाबदेह ना होना, क्योंकि उसकी मानसिकता तानाशाही होना – गुलिवर का घोड़ों के स्वामी को भ्रष्ट राजनीति के विषय में बताना।

Ans. Gulliver presented the exact picture of politics as it existed in England which was a shocking experience for the master horse because the politics of England was fully deviated from its actual purpose.

Gulliver discussed the characteristic requisites which were required for any person to be a Chief Minister in the Government and he accepted that sanctimoniousness was the most prominently required feature.

He further told the master horse that if someone defamed the court, he would be choosen as Chief Minister because he would prove always flattering and submissive throughout his service period.

A person elected in such way could not do anything progressive for the nation or society because of various restrictions and greed of saving his position and power.

Such ministers were not answerable to the public because of their dictatorship and finally the public had to suffer. Gulliver told the master horse that the politics of England was also corrupt and ineffective like other aspects.

Introduction

Gulliver expresses his desire not to return to human society. The master horse compares Yahoos and humans and concludes that both are similar to a great extent.

Similarities between Yahoos and Human Beings

The master horse comments that although a Yahoo appears to be gifted with a small amount of reason, he only misuses it to degrade himself. Besides, a man lacks all those natural characteristics possessed by a Yahoo, such as quickness.

Yahoos and the humans rebel and dispute among themselves for the same reasons, e.g. both are greedy. Yahoos fight their neighbours unnecessarily and if they have no foe, they start fighting amongst themselves. Yahoos consume an intoxicating root while humans consume wine. Yahoos, like humans, are subject to illnesses of excess. He falls a prey to the hatred of his fellow Yahoos.

The master horse says that a Yahoo habitually sits and howls in a corner unnecessarily. So, a Yahoo is fit to do hard work. Gulliver calls this a disease known as spleen from which the wealthy and idle Englishmen are afflicted.

Word Meaning

Congruity	– सामंजस्य	Prevail	– जीतना
Incitement	– भड़कावा	Bias	– पक्षपात
Conjecture	– अनुमान लगाना	Gross	– कुल योग
Odiousness	– आक्रामकता	Deformity	– अंग विकृति

परिचय

Gulliver (गुलिवर) अपने समाज में दोबारा न लौटने की इच्छा व्यक्त करता है। घोड़ों का स्वामी याहू प्राणियों एवं मनुष्यों में तुलना करता है तथा उसे दोनों में अत्यधिक समता नजर आती है।

याहू प्राणियों एवं मनुष्यों में समानताएँ

घोड़ों का स्वामी कहता है कि यद्यपि एक Yahoo (याहू) प्राणी को प्राकृतिक रूप से तर्कशक्ति मिली होती है, फिर भी वह उसका प्रयोग स्वयं की हानि करने में करता है। इसके अतिरिक्त, एक मनुष्य में कई प्रकार की कमियाँ होती हैं; जैसे-एक याहू प्राणी अत्यंत तीव्र होता है।

याहू प्राणी एवं मनुष्य आपस में समान कारणों से ही लड़ाइयाँ भी करते हैं और दोनों ही लोभी स्वभाव के होते हैं। याहू प्राणी अपने पड़ोसियों से लड़ते हैं तथा यदि उनका कोई शत्रु नहीं होता है तो वे स्वयं आपस में लड़ाइयाँ प्रारंभ कर देते हैं। याहू प्राणी एक प्रकार की नशा उत्पन्न करने वाली जड़ों को खाते हैं, जबकि मनुष्य शराब का सेवन करते हैं। मनुष्यों की ही भाँति याहू प्राणी भी बहुधा बीमार होते हैं।

याहू प्राणी अपनी आदत के अनुसार किनारे बैठकर अनावश्यक रूप से हंगामा करते रहते हैं; अत: एक याहू प्राणी कठोर परिश्रम वाले कार्यों हेतु उपयुक्त होता है। गुलिवर बताता है कि इस प्रकार की बीमारी England (इंग्लैंड) में भी होती है।

Sordid	– अनैतिक	Contending	– विरोधी मुद्रा में
Equity	– न्याय	Stealth	– गुपचुप तरीके से
Tumble	– अचानक गिरना	Plundering	– लूटमार, युद्ध

Important Questions

Questions based on the Plot of the Chapter

Q 1. Why was Gulliver not ready to return to his country?

गुलिवर अपने देश वापस जाने हेतु क्यों राजी नहीं था?

↗ गुलिवर का एक समझदार व्यक्ति होना – उसका अपने समाज में जारी कुरीतियों से असंतुष्ट रहना – गुलिवर का उन्हें बदलने हेतु व्याकुल होना – गुलिवर का घोड़ों की दुनिया को समझना तथा उसे पसंद करना – घोड़ों के स्वामी का व्यवहार गुलिवर को अत्यधिक पसंद आना – घोड़ों के प्रति गुलिवर का लगाव बढ़ जाना – गुलिवर का भ्रष्टाचार कर्त्तव्य विमुखता के विरुद्ध होना – उसका उस दुनिया में रहने हेतु लालायित हो जाना – लेकिन व्यावहारिक रूप से यह उसके लिए मुश्किल होना – गुलिवर का कोई निर्णय ले सकने में अक्षम होना।

Ans. Gulliver was a sincere person and he was completely unsatisfied with the bad practices of his society. Gulliver wanted to change them because those bad practices were harmful for the society and people were much troubled because of those bad practices. Gulliver observed the environment and society structure of horses which he found fair enough. Except this, the master horse behaved in a very co-operative way with Gulliver, so Gulliver felt an affection for all the horses.

Gulliver was totally against of corruption, deviation from duties and so on. Conclusively, it can be said that Gulliver began to like the straight and plain environment of the island of horses which induced him to stay there with those horses.

However, he had a family in England, so practically it was a little bit tough for him to take decision of staying there.

Q 2. How did the master horse contrast and compare the Yahoos and human beings? Describe regarding both females and males.

घोड़ों के स्वामी ने याहू प्राणियों एवं मानवों में क्या समानताएँ एवं विषमताएँ बताईं? नर एवं मादा दोनों के संदर्भ में वर्णन करिए।

घोड़ों के स्वामी का याहू एवं मनुष्यों में तुलना करना – दोनों समूहों में अत्यधिक समानता होना – याहू प्राणियों की तर्कशक्ति बेहतर होना, परंतु उनके द्वारा इसका उचित उपयोग न करना – दोनों समूहों का स्वभाव लड़ाकू होना – याहू प्राणियों का अपनी संपत्ति की सुरक्षा को लेकर चिंतित रहना – याहू प्राणी एवं मनुष्य दोनों में बीमार पड़ने की प्रवृत्ति का विद्यमान होना – याहू प्राणियों के समूह का एक भद्दे याहू द्वारा संचालित किया जाना – याहू प्राणियों का परिश्रम हेतु उपयुक्त होना – घोड़ों के स्वामी का गुलिवर को मादा याहू प्राणियों की विचित्र आदतें बताना।

Ans. The master horse presented an overall comparison between the Yahoos and human beings and tried to conclude that there were a lot of similarities between both the groups. The master horse explained that Yahoos had more reasoning skills, but they could never use it for their benefits because of their nature.

Further, the master horse said that both groups had disputes among themselves for almost same reasons as both were greedy. The Yahoos believed in collecting gems in a large amount, but they were always doubtful regarding safety and security of their possession.

The Yahoos consumed an intoxicating root whereas humans consumed wine for the same purpose. The Yahoos and human beings, both were subject to illnesses and weaknesses.

The master horse explained a different thing about the Yahoos that each herd of Yahoos was led by uglier and more ill behaved Yahoo than his fellows. In addition to this, the Yahoos were fit for hard work. The master horse told Gulliver about the strange habits of the female Yahoos.

Gulliver Studies the Yahoos

Gulliver seeks the master horse's permission to go among the Yahoos and study them. Gulliver wants to see if they really resemble humans. On the other hand, they believe that Gulliver is one of them. Gulliver comes across a crying three-year-old Yahoo child. Gulliver finds that the child is emitting a fox like smell.

गुलिवर का याहू प्राणियों का विश्लेषण करना

Gulliver (गुलिवर) घोड़ों के स्वामी से आज्ञा लेकर याहू प्राणियों का विश्लेषण आरंभ कर देता है। गुलिवर यह जानना चाहता है कि क्या याहू प्राणी वास्तव में मनुष्यों की भाँति दिखते हैं। इसके विपरीत उनकी यह अवधारणा थी कि गुलिवर भी उनमें से एक है। गुलिवर को इस दौरान एक तीन वर्षीय याहू बालक नजर आता है जो विलाप कर रहा है। गुलिवर अनुभव करता है कि बालक के शरीर से Fox (लोमड़ी) की गंध जैसी आ रही है। इसके पश्चात् बालक गुलिवर के वस्त्रों पर अपशिष्ट पदार्थ का त्याग कर देता है

Matrimony

While making matrimonial matches, the Houyhnhnms consider the strength and vigor of the race as a whole. They are not aware of courtship or romantic love, but the couple demonstrates the same generosity and veneration to each other as to the rest of their race. The Houyhnhnms apply their rules of reason even to marriage, which is always arranged for a couple by their parents. Houyhnhnm couples are always faithful.

वैवाहिक रीतियाँ

वैवाहिक रिश्ते बनाते समय Houyhnhnms (हायोम्स) संपूर्ण प्रजाति की संख्या एवं अन्य बातों का ध्यान रखते हैं। वे प्रेम विवाह अथवा गुप्त विवाह की धारणा में विश्वास नहीं करते हैं परंतु विवाहित दंपति एक- दूसरे का सम्मान किया करते हैं तथा पूरी प्रजाति के साथ समान प्रकार का व्यवहार करते हैं। हायोम्स विवाह के रिश्तों में भी संस्कारों का पालन करते हैं तथा वैवाहिक रिश्ते माता-पिता द्वारा ही निर्धारित किए जाते हैं। हायोम दंपति एक-दूसरे के प्रति Faithful (वफादार) होते हैं।

Word Meaning

Pestered	– परेशान	Rank	– तीक्ष्ण गंध वाला
Presence	– उपस्थिति	Perverse	– जिद्दी
Insolent	– दुष्ट	Revengeful	– बदले की भावना से युक्त
Restive	– काबू से बाहर	Stark	– पूर्णतः
Mortification	– शर्मिंदगी	Propensity	– प्राकृतिक झुकाव
Consorts	– पति या पत्नी	Comeliness	– सुंदरता
Temperance	– मादक पदार्थों का त्याग	Brutality	– क्रूरता

Important Questions

Questions based on the Plot of the Chapter

Q 1. What did Gulliver study about the Yahoos? What did he conclude?

गुलिवर ने याहू प्राणियों के विषय में क्या अध्ययन किया? इस आधार पर उसने क्या निष्कर्ष निकाले?

गुलिवर का हायोम्स एवं याहू प्राणियों के विभिन्न पक्षों को उजागर करना – दोनों जातियों को एक-दूसरे से पूर्णतः भिन्न पाना – गुलिवर का याहू प्राणियों का सूक्ष्म अं-वेषण करना तथा उनकी तुलना मनुष्यों से करना – याहू प्राणियों का स्वभावतः उग्र होना – गुलिवर का याहू प्राणियों के संबंध में कई निष्कर्ष निकालना, जैसे - उनकी गंध अरुचिकर होना – उन प्राणियों का दुष्ट एवं आक्रामक होना – उनका अव्यवस्थित रहना, उन्हें कुछ सिखाना अत्यंत दुरूह होना – उनका ऊपरी तौर पर कठोर एवं अंदरूनी तौर पर कायर होना – उनका लोभी एवं द्वेषपूर्ण होना।

Ans. Gulliver describes various particulars of the Yahoos and Houyhnhnms because he found both groups totally different from each other. After the permission of the master horse, Gulliver observed the Yahoos carefully and tried to compare them with humans. However, he had to become very careful during his observation because all Yahoos were quite offensive and rude and he had no sword at that time.

Gulliver saw a three year old baby and he experienced that the smell of that baby was quite obnoxious. On the basis of his observation, Gulliver reached various conclusions like the smell of Yahoos was very offensive, there sight was quite abominable.

It was very tough to teach them and they were quite unwilling to be controlled, they were strong and hard, but internally they were too weak, they were rude as well as lustful, they were worthless, etc. Gulliver got almost every detail related to Yahoos and this proved helpful in understanding the Yahoos.

Q 2. What was the matrimonial system in the Houyhnhnm society?

हायोम समाज में विवाह की क्या पद्धति थी?

गुलिवर का हायोम्स की दुनिया को देखना तथा वहाँ व्याप्त अनुशासन को देखकर प्रसन्न हो जाना – विवाह की पद्धति का पूर्णतः सामान्य होना – विवाह के दौरान मुख्य रूप से नर में 'ताकत' एवं मादा में 'खूबसूरती' की बारीकी से जाँच किया जाना – प्रेम विवाह या गुप्त विवाह का समर्थन न किया जाना – विवाह के दौरान वर-वधू के समान जाति से संबंधित होने पर विशेष जोर दिया जाना – रूढ़िवादी परंपराएँ निभाया जाना – वैवाहिक जिम्मेदारियाँ एवं आयोजन संबंधी समस्याओं को मुख्य रूप से वर-वधू के माता-पिता द्वारा हल किया जाना।

Ans. Gulliver observed the world of the horses and he became fully surprised because he found there extreme accuracy and a good quality discipline. Houyhnhnms used to follow their strict rules in almost every aspect of their society and even a slight deviation was not tolerable there.

The matrimonial system of the world of the horses was quite simple and they considered the strength and vigor of the race as a whole during the decisions of marriages. The main virtue which was observed in males was 'strength' and same in females was 'comeliness'. They did not believe in courtship or romantic love and the couple behaved well with the rest of the society. They did not believe in mixing races, so only same colour marriage was allowed there.

They used to follow conventional pattern and everything was arranged for any couple by their parents. Those couples were very faithful for sake of their happy and successful married life.

Question based on the Character Sketch

Q 3. On the basis of this chapter, give a brief character sketch of the Houyhnhnms.

अध्याय के आधार पर हायोम्स के चरित्र की विशेषताओं का संक्षिप्त वर्णन करिए।

हायोम्स का सज्जन एवं सद्गुणी होना – उनका बुरी आदतों से दूर होना – हायोम्स का ईमानदार एवं अनुशासित होना – अपने समाज में किसी प्रकार की बुराई को पनपने का अवसर न देना – अपने समाज को आदर्श बनाने में कामयाब होना – हायोम्स का प्रगतिवादी जानवर होना – जाति या लिंग आधारित भेद न करना – इस प्रकार हायोम्स का ईमानदार, अनुशासनप्रिय एवं प्रगतिवादी होना।

Ans. The Houyhnhnms were very upright and virtuous because they never followed any type of bad practices.
On the basis of this chapter, we see following traits in their characters

Honest and Disciplined The Houyhnhnms were very honest and disciplined because they never adopted or promoted any bad practice in their society. They wanted to make their society like heaven and they were quite successful in their mission because there was no discrepancy in their society.

Progressive Animals The Houyhnhnms were progressive animals because they never believed in any kind of biasing on the basis of gender or any other factor. They were in favour of equal rights and opportunities for all sexes.
Thus, it can be said that the Hauyhnhnms were honest, disciplined and progressive animals.

9

The Houyhnhnms Hold their Grand Assembly

The Houyhnhnms hold one of their grand assemblies and discuss if the Yahoos should be wiped out from the face of the earth as the Yahoos trample the Houyhnhnms, crops and steal their milk. In the meantime, the Houyhnhnms could start to domesticate asses.

The Houyhnhnm Society in General

The Houyhnhnm society has no written language. They rely on oral records for their history. They believe in practical astronomy. They measure months and years.

They write beautiful poetry about friendship and in praise of their athletes. Unless they have some kind of accident, they only die of old age, usually at around 70 or 75. Their friends and relatives are neither sad nor joyous at their death as the philosophy behind it is their belief that death is simply a return to the first mother.

The Houyhnhnms are Excessively Disgusted with the Yahoos

The Houyhnhnms are so disgusted with the Yahoos that all of their words for something bad are connected to Yahoos, so a poorly built house is 'ynholmhmrohlnw yahoo' and a stone that cuts their feet, 'ynlhmndwihlma yahoo'. The Houyhnhnmw are unable to express anything evil. They describe mistakes or unpleasant events by adding the word 'Yahoo' to the word or phrase.

हायोम्स का अपनी भव्य सभा का आयोजन करना

Houyhrhnms (हायोम्स) अपने साथियों के साथ एक सभा का आयोजन करते हैं, जिसमें वे चर्चा करते हैं कि धरती से याहू प्राणियों का नामोनिशान मिटा देना चाहिए, क्योंकि याहू प्राणी हायोम्स की फसलों को नष्ट कर दिया करते हैं एवं दूध की चोरी कर लेते हैं। उस समय हायोम्स गधों को पालतू बनाने के विषय में विचार करते हैं।

हायोम समाज के सामान्य नियम

हायोम समाज में लेखन की कोई भाषा प्रचलन में नहीं हुआ करती है। वे अपने History (इतिहास) एवं इससे जुड़ी जानकारियों हेतु मौखिक आँकड़ों पर निर्भर रहते हैं। वे व्यावहारिक खगोल विज्ञान में विश्वास करते हैं। वे महीनों एवं वर्षों की गणना करते हैं।

वे मित्रता के विषय में बहुत उच्च कोटि की कविताएँ लिखा करते हैं तथा अपने व्यायामी साथियों की प्रशंसा में भी लिखा करते हैं। यदि किसी प्रकार की दुर्घटना न हो, तो वे वृद्धावस्था को प्राप्त होने के पश्चात् ही लगभग 70 से 75 वर्ष की आयु में ही मृत्यु को प्राप्त होते हैं। उनकी मृत्यु होने पर उनके परिजन न ही शोक व्यक्त करते हैं और न ही हर्ष व्यक्त करते हैं, क्योंकि इसके पीछे उनकी इस धारणा का हाथ है कि मृत्यु केवल प्रथम माता के पास लौट जाने का नाम होती है।

हायोम्स का याहू प्राणियों से घृणा करना

हायोम्स याहू प्राणियों से इस कदर घृणा करते हैं कि उनसे जुड़े किसी भी अप्रिय विषय के नाम को वे याहू प्राणियों से जोड़ दिया करते हैं। अत: यदि कोई घर अत्यंत लापरवाही के साथ बनाया हुआ होता है तो वे उसे Ynholmhmrohlnm Yahoo ('यनहोमरोन याहू') का नाम देते हैं तथा इसी प्रकार यदि कोई पत्थर उनका पैर जख्मी कर दे तो वे उसे Ynlhmndwihlma Yahoo ('यनहमनड्विल्मा याहू') का नाम देते हैं। हायोम्स किसी भी प्रकार की बुराई को व्यक्त करने में अक्षम हैं। वे गलतियों या अरुचिकर स्थितियों को व्यक्त करने हेतु शब्द या वाक्यांश में Yahoo ('याहू') जोड़ दिया करते हैं, जिससे उनका उद्देश्य पूर्ण हो जाता है।

Word Meaning

Indocible	– उद्दंड	Devour	– भक्षण करना
Brood	– संतान	Expedient	– उपाय
Forsaken	– पूर्णतया परित्यक्त	Companion	– साथी
Tincture	– रंग	Tractable	– सरल स्वभाव वाला
Maim	– अपंग करना	Virtue	– गुण
Inimitable	– अनुकरणीय, अनोखा	Flint	– एक प्रकार का पत्थर
Obscurest	– अज्ञात	Wooden	– लकड़ी का
Language	– भाषा		

Important Questions

Questions based on the Plot of the Chapter

Q 1. What were the topics discussed at the grand assembly of the Houyhnhnms?

हायोम्स ने विशाल सभा में किन-किन मुद्दों पर चर्चा की?

हायोम्स का अपने समाज की सुरक्षा के प्रति चिंतित होना – उनके द्वारा अपने समाज को बेहतर बनाने हेतु सतत प्रयास करना – समय-समय पर उनके द्वारा उनकी नीतियों की समीक्षा होना – उनके द्वारा एक विशाल सभा का आयोजन किया जाना – जिसमें उनके द्वारा विभिन्न मुद्दों पर चर्चा किया जाना – याहू प्राणियों का उनके लिए मुसीबत का सबब बन जाना – हायोम्स का याहू प्राणियों को चिकित्सा द्वारा नपुंसक एवं ओजहीन बनाने के विषय में सोचना – हायोम्स का याहू प्राणियों से छुटकारा पाने हेतु व्यग्र होना।

Ans. The Houyhnhnms were very much concerned about the safety and security of their society because the society was the resultant of their continuous sacrifice and hard work. They used to discuss various aspects and this provided them to review their rules and regulations in order to bring more prosperity and betterness. When they headed towards their grand assembly, they had various issues for discussion. They discussed whether they should wipe out the Yahoos from the face of the earth as the Yahoos were being very troublesome for them.

The Yahoos used to trample the crops of the Houyhnhnms and except this, they used to steal the milk of the Houyhnhnm cows.

The Houyhnhnms thought that they should castrate the Yahoos in order to make them helpless and weak without killing them. The Houyhnhnms were very disturbed because of the Yahoos and that's why they were framing a lot of plans in order to get rid from the Yahoos anyhow.

Q 2. Explain the society and general traditions regarding Houyhnhnms.

हायोम्स के संदर्भ में समाज एवं सामान्य परंपराओं की व्याख्या करिए।

हायोम्स के समाज का भिन्न होना, क्योंकि उनके द्वारा कुछ निश्चित सिद्धांतों का पालन किया जाना – उनके समाज में कुछ सामान्य रीति-रिवाजों का पाया जाना – उनके समाज में लिखने की कोई सर्वमान्य भाषा का न होना – उनका खगोलशास्त्र में विश्वास करना तथा त्रुटिरहित गणनाएँ करना – उनका मित्रता पर कविताएँ लिखना तथा व्यायामी साथियों के विषय में भी बहुत कुछ लिखना – अधिकांश हायोम्स का प्राकृतिक रूप से ही मृत्यु को प्राप्त होना – उनका किसी की मृत्यु पर कोई प्रतिक्रिया न प्रदर्शित करना – मृत्यु के विषय में उनकी मान्यता अलग प्रकार की होना।

Ans. The society of the Houyhnhnms was quite different because they had some set of rules and regulations which were strictly followed by them. The society of the Houyhnhnms was nothing but the resultant of dedication of its residents towards their values and principles. However, there were some general but exceptional traditions in their society as they had no written language in their society. The Houyhnhnms relied only on oral records for their history.

They were a firm believer of practical astronomy and they were very quick and exact in time related calculation. Except this, they used to write beautiful poetry about friendship and they were very generous towards their athletes also as per the writing was concerned.

They had average life span of 70 to 75 years and they did not meet with any type of unnatural death except a very few cases. They used to show no reaction on deaths because they believed in the theory that death is nothing but the process of returning to the first mother.

Q 3. How it can be said that the Yahoos were hated by the Houyhnhnms?

यह कैसे कहा जा सकता है कि हायोम्स याहू प्राणियों से नफरत करते थे?

हायोम्स द्वारा जीवन को बेहतर प्रकार से जीने की कोशिश किया जाना – जबकि याहू प्राणियों द्वारा गलत आदतें अपनाया जाना – हायोम्स द्वारा याहू प्राणियों के समापन के विषय में सोचा जाना, क्योंकि याहू प्राणियों का निकम्मा होना – याहू प्राणियों का असभ्य होना – हायोम्य द्वारा विभिन्न प्रकार की योजना बनाया जाना, जिससे उन्हें याहू प्राणियों से छुटकारा मिल सके – याहू प्राणियों से हायोम्स की नफरत बढ़ती जाना – हायोम्स का प्राकृतिक रूप से बुराई को व्यक्त करने में असमर्थ होना – उनके द्वारा 'याहू' शब्द का प्रयोग बुराई के प्रतीक के रूप में किया जाना – याहू प्राणियों का वास्तव में असभ्य एवं घृणा का पात्र होना।

Ans. The Houyhnhnms believed in living life in the best possible virtuous way whereas the Yahoos lived their life in a detestable manner, so the Yahoos were hated by the Houyhnhnms. The Houyhnhnms followed the best practices and they always supported positive things, but the Yahoos had every bad quality which was the biggest reason for their bad condition.

The Houyhnhnms wanted to wipe out the Yahoos from the face of the earth because they found them extremely troublesome and worthless. Except this, the Yahoos were not civilized which was also an issue for the Houyhnhnms. The Houyhnhnms used to frame various plans in order to get rid from the Yahoos because they did not want to tolerate them.

The Houyhnhnms were not able to express anything evil, so they used to adopt the term 'Yahoo' as a filler when they had to express something evil or unpleasant. The Houyhnhnms disliked everything related to the Yahoos and that's why they used this technique in order to express their hate for them. However, the Yahoos were really very rude and uncivilised.

Question based on the Character Sketch

Q 4. On the basis of this chapter, give a brief character sketch of Houyhnhnms.

अध्याय के आधार पर हायोम्स का संक्षिप्त चरित्र चित्रण करिए।

हायोम्स का ईमानदार एवं अनुशासनप्रिय होना – उनका याहू प्राणियों को नापसंद करना – हायोम्स का सतत उन्नति हेतु प्रयत्नशील होना – उत्कृष्ट नियम-कानून बनाने का प्रयास करना एवं उसे लागू करना जिससे उनकी दुनिया और समृद्ध हो जाए – हायोम्स का याहू प्राणियों से नफरत करना – याहू प्राणियों का अविश्वसनीय, असभ्य, व्यर्थ एवं परेशानी उत्पन्न करने वाला होना – हायोम्स द्वारा उनका समापन चाहना।

Ans. The Houyhnhnms were very honest and fair, but they were very strict in case of discipline also. However, they did not like the Yahoos because of the bad habits of the Yahoos.

On the basis of this chapter, we see following traits in their characteristics

Striving for progress The Houyhnhnms were very hard working and they were not satisfied with their status, that's why they strived for progress always. They wanted to implement better rules and regulations so that they could make their surroundings more errorfree and pleasant for living.

Disdain for Yahoos The Houyhnhnms were heavily disdainful for the Yahoos because they simply disliked the habits of Yahoos. The Yahoos were quite disgusting, unfaithful, useless and disturbing in nature. The Houyhnhnms wanted to wipe them out even from the face of the earth.

Thus, we can say that the Houyhnhnms were striving for progress and disdainful for Yahoos.

Introduction

Gulliver is happy among the Houyhnhnms. Suddenly, he is asked by the master horse to leave the country. Gulliver is shocked and finally, he is given a farewell.

Gulliver Settles Down among the Houyhnhnms

The master horse orders a room to be prepared for Gulliver. He plasters the room with clay and covers with rushmats. He also prepares a bed and two chairs. He designs new clothes from the skins of rabbits and also new stockings. Gulliver eats honey with bread. He enjoys perfect health of body and calmness of mind.

There is no disloyalty of a friend, injuries of a secret or enemy or any other evil. He is not surrounded by hypocrites or liars but friends who are absolutely virtuous. He praises them for their strength, beauty and speed. He has developed in himself their speaking and walking manners. He is proud to run like a horse. He is absolute happy and content on the island. Infact, he enjoys the life as he had never done in the past.

Gulliver is Asked to Leave

The other Houyhnhnms are anxious about the presence of a Yahoo among them. They are scared lest such a smart person should rebel against them. They convey their fears and worries to the master horse. They also instigate him to ask Gulliver to leave the island. The master horse approaches Gulliver that it has been decided at their general assembly that he should either leave the island or work as a Yahoo.

10

परिचय

Gulliver (गुलिवर) Houyhnhnms (हायोम्स) के साथ प्रसन्नतापूर्वक रह रहा है। अचानक एक दिन घोड़ों का स्वामी उसे द्वीप छोड़कर लौटने को कहता है। यह सुनकर गुलिवर आश्चर्यचकित रह जाता है और अंततः गुलिवर लौटने हेतु राजी हो जाता है तथा उसे विदाई दी जाती है।

गुलिवर का हायोम्स के साथ घुल-मिल जाना

घोड़ों का स्वामी गुलिवर के लिए एक कमरा बनाने का आदेश देता है। वह कमरे का मिट्टी से लेप करवाता है तथा कमरे को उच्च कोटि की चटाइयों से सजवाता है। वह कमरे में एक पलंग तथा दो Chairs (कुर्सियाँ) भी रखवा देता है। वह खरगोश की त्वचा से बेहतरीन मुलायम कपड़े तथा मोजे बनवाता है। गुलिवर को ब्रेड एवं शहद खाने हेतु दिया जाता है।

उसे अच्छा स्वास्थ्य तथा मानसिक सुकून दोनों ही प्राप्त होते हैं। यहाँ किसी प्रकार का धोखा, दुश्मन से खतरा या किसी अन्य प्रकार की हानि नहीं है। वह वहाँ पर झूठे एवं दिखावापसंद लोगों के साथ नहीं अपितु कुछ सर्वश्रेष्ठ एवं सद्गुणी लोगों के साथ है। वह उन हायोम्स की उनके गुणों ; जैसे– ताकत, सुंदरता तथा तीव्रता के कारण उनकी प्रशंसा करता है। वह स्वयं को उनके बोलने के अंदाज व चाल-ढाल के अनुरूप ढाल लेता है। उसे घोड़ों की भाँति दौड़ने में गर्व की अनुभूति होती है। वह उस द्वीप पर पूर्ण आनंद एवं संतोष प्राप्त करता है। वास्तव में उसे जितना आनंद उस द्वीप पर आने लगता है उतना पूर्व में कभी नहीं आया था।

गुलिवर को द्वीप छोड़ने को कहा जाना

सभी हायोम्स इस बात को लेकर थोड़े शंकित हैं कि उनके मध्य एक याहू प्राणी उपस्थित है। उन्हें इस बात की शंका है कि याहू चालाक होते हैं। अतः वे उनके खिलाफ बगावत कर सकते हैं। वे अपनी सारी चिंताएँ तथा भय घोड़ों के स्वामी को बताते हैं। वे स्वामी को गुलिवर को Island (द्वीप) छोड़कर जाने का आदेश देने के लिए भी भड़काते हैं। घोड़ों का स्वामी गुलिवर को कहता है कि आम सहमति में सबने निर्णय लिया है कि उसे द्वीप को छोड़ना होगा अथवा याहू प्राणियों की भाँति कार्य करना होगा।

Gulliver Leaves

Finally, when the day comes for Gulliver to leave, the master horse and his whole family come to see him off. Panicky and dejected, he sets sail, but before leaving he kisses the hoof of the master horse.

गुलिवर का द्वीप छोड़ देना

अंततः जब गुलिवर विदा होने लगता है तब घोड़ों का स्वामी अपने पूरे परिवार के साथ उसे विदाई देने आ जाता है। इसके पश्चात् निराश एवं दु:खी मुद्रा में गुलिवर विदा लेता है तथा जाने से पूर्व वह घोड़ों के स्वामी के खुरों का चुंबन लेता है।

Word Meaning

Content	– संतोष	Necessity	– आवश्यकता
Tranquility	– शांति	Inconstancy	– धोखेबाजी
Minion	– सहयोगी	Buffoon	– विदूषक
Bawd	– वेश्या	Dungeon	– कारागार
Fiddler	– सारंगी वादक	Sentiment	– भावुकता
Folly	– मूर्खता	Perplexity	– हैरानी
Exhortation	– दबाव	Distance	– दूरी

Important Questions

Questions based on the Plot of the Chapter

Q 1. How can you say that Gulliver was extremely comfortable among the horses?

यह किस प्रकार कहा जा सकता है कि गुलिवर घोड़ों के साथ अत्यंत सुविधापूर्वक था?

गुलिवर का घोड़ों के साथ प्रसन्नतापूर्वक रहना तथा सुरक्षित अनुभव करना – घोड़ों के स्वामी का व्यवहार अत्यंत उत्तम होना – घोड़ों के स्वामी द्वारा गुलिवर के लिए विभिन्न प्रकार के प्रबंध कराए जाना – गुलिवर हेतु एक सुसज्जित कमरा उपलब्ध कराया जाना – उसे नए आरामदेह कपड़े उपलब्ध कराया जाना – उत्तम प्रकृति का भोजन दिया जाना – गुलिवर का जिंदगी के प्रत्येक क्षण का लुत्फ उठाना – वहाँ उसका मानसिक रूप से स्वतंत्र होना, क्योंकि वहाँ उसके शत्रुओं का न होना – गुलिवर का सुविधाओं का आनंद उठाना – इस प्रकार उसका प्रसन्न एवं संतुष्ट रहना।

Ans. Gulliver was living with the horses and this was a better experience for him as he felt quite safe himself there. Except this, the behaviour of the master horse was very co-operative and caring towards him which was a comfortable feeling for him. The master horse made various arrangements for him as a separate room was prepared for him which was fully furnished and decorated, new clothes were made for him, better quality food was served to him, no burden was given to him, etc.

However, Gulliver enjoyed his life very much during his stay with the horses. There he was freeminded because no one was there to cheat him or disturb him as the horses were very much judicious and pacific in their approach. Gulliver enjoyed every moment of his life because all facilities were present there for him. Thus, we can say that Gulliver was comfortable among the horses.

Q 2. What were the things that always disturbed Gulliver but not while he was among the Houyhnhnms?

कौन-सी बातें गुलिवर को परेशान किया करती थीं, परंतु हायोम्स के साथ रहते हुए उसे उन बातों से कोई परेशानी नहीं होती थी?

गुलिवर मानव समाज का हिस्सा था, जिसका विभिन्न प्रकार की बुराइयों से परिपूर्ण होना – गुलिवर का सभी प्रकार की बुराइयों के खिलाफ होना – गुलिवर का औरों द्वारा किए गए षड्यंत्रों का सामना करने हेतु विवश होना – घोड़ों के द्वीप पर पहुँचकर गुलिवर को अत्यंत सुखद अनुभव होना, क्योंकि वहाँ शांति होना – विभिन्न प्रकार के दुर्गुणों से उस द्वीप का मुक्त होना – गुलिवर को वहाँ दिखावापसंद लोग, लोभी या धोखेबाज न मिलना – वहाँ के निवासियों का सद्गुणों से युक्त होना – गुलिवर का वहाँ बसने का निर्णय लेना, परंतु बाद में अप्रत्याशित कारणों से उसका द्वीप छोड़कर जाना।

Ans. Gulliver lived in human society which was full of various types of bad practices and Gulliver did not like this. Any bad practice was not followed by Gulliver, but he had to face various types of conspiracies by others for himself. Gulliver found a lot of drawbacks in human society, but when he entered the island of horses, he began to feel good because the society of the horses was quite free from such types of bad practices.

Gulliver became very happy because he got a totally different environment there as there was no one to cheat him, there was no hypocrite, there was no liar, the residents were absolutely virtuous there, etc. The environment of that island was very pleasant and interesting for Gulliver. Gulliver decided to stay there permanently, but later he had to leave the island because of some unexpected factors.

Introduction

Gulliver provides a narrative of his dangerous voyage. He arrives at New-Holland hoping to settle there. He is wounded with an arrow by one of the natives. He is seized and carried by force into a Portuguese ship. The kind behaviour of the captain is narrated. Gulliver arrives at England though reluctantly.

Gulliver is Wounded

Much against his will, sad and depressed, Gulliver begins his voyage. Gulliver paddles away from the shore, determined not to go very far from the Houyhnhnms. The master horse and the Houyhnhnms continue on the shores unless Gulliver disappears from their sight. The sorrel nag bids him the final farewell telling him to take care of himself. Gulliver is looking for an uninhabited island which can furnish him the necessities of life. He discovers a small island and stays there for four days on raw oysters and limpets.

On the fourth day, he comes across the natives stark naked and sitting around a fire. Gulliver runs to his canoe and rows away, but not before he is shot in his left knee with a poisoned arrow, which leaves a scar.

Gulliver Sees a Portuguese Ship

Gulliver sees a Portuguese ship, but as he can not afford to share a ship with the Yahoos, he decides to return to another side of the island. The sailors land and find Gulliver. They address Gulliver in Portuguese and Gulliver replies that he is a poor Yahoos exiled from the land of the Houyhnhnms. He is reluctant to leave, but the sailors bring Gulliver aboard their ship heading for Lisbon in Portugal.

11

परिचय

गुलिवर अपनी खतरनाक समुद्री यात्रा का वर्णन करता है। वह New Holland (न्यू हॉलैंड) पहुँच जाता है, जहाँ वह बसने का मन बना लेता है। वह वहाँ के व्यक्ति द्वारा तीर चलाए जाने पर घायल हो जाता है। उसे जबरन बंदी बना लिया जाता है तथा एक पुर्तगाली जहाज पर ले जाया जाता है। जहाज के कप्तान का व्यवहार अच्छा है। गुलिवर अनिच्छा से England (इंग्लैंड) पहुँच जाता है।

गुलिवर का जख्मी हो जाना

गुलिवर भारी मन से तथा अनिच्छापूर्वक अपनी समुद्री यात्रा प्रारंभ करता है। गुलिवर किनारे से कुछ ही दूर जाता है, क्योंकि वह Houyhnhnms (हायोम्स) से अधिक दूर नहीं जाना चाहता। घोड़ों का स्वामी तथा अन्य सभी हायोम्स किनारे पर तब तक मौजूद रहते हैं जब तक गुलिवर उनकी आँखों से ओझल नहीं हो जाता। हल्के रंग का घोड़ा उसे खुद का ख्याल रखने को कहकर उसे अंतिम विदाई देता है। गुलिवर एक निर्जन द्वीप की तलाश करने लगता है जहाँ उसकी सारी आवश्यकताएँ पूरी हो सकें। वह एक छोटे से द्वीप पर चार दिनों तक रुकता है तथा इस दौरान वह घोंघे खाकर गुजारा करता है।

चौथे दिन उसे उस द्वीप का एक निवासी नजर आता है, जो बिल्कुल नग्न था तथा आग के निकट बैठा था। गुलिवर दौड़कर अपनी नौका पर जाता है तथा भागने का प्रयत्न करने लगता है, परंतु उसके बाएँ घुटने में जहरीले तीर से वार किया जाता है, जो उसके घुटने पर निशान छोड़ देता है।

गुलिवर को पुर्तगाली जहाज नजर आना

गुलिवर को एक पुर्तगाली जहाज नजर आता है, परंतु उसे याहू प्राणियों के साथ यात्रा में कोई दिलचस्पी नहीं थी अत: वह द्वीप के दूसरे किनारे पर जाने का निर्णय लेता है। नाविक आते हैं तथा गुलिवर को ढूँढ लेते हैं। वे गुलिवर से Portuguese (पुर्तगाली) भाषा में संवाद करते हुए उससे उसके विषय में पूछते हैं, तो गुलिवर उन्हें बताता है कि वह एक निरीह याहू प्राणी है जिसे हायोम्स ने देश निकाला की सजा दी है। यद्यपि गुलिवर जाने की मुद्रा में नहीं है, परंतु नाविक उसे अपने जहाज पर बैठा लेते हैं, जो Lisbon (लिस्बन) की तरफ जा रहा था।

The captain, Don Pedro de Mendez, is a nice gentleman and very benevolent towards Gulliver. He wants to know Gulliver's whereabouts but Gulliver, extremely overpowered by his hatred for the Yahoos, will not disclose him anything. Nor can he afford to stand near Yahoos, so during most of the voyages, he remains confined to his cabin. He tries to dive into the sea to swim away, but he is caught. Don Pedro does not believe Gulliver's story of the Houyhnhnm land, but Gulliver has not heard a lie since long. Gulliver promises the captain not to commit suicide while returning home. In Lisbon, Don Pedro wants Gulliver to stay with him. After ten days in Portugal, Don Pedro reminds Gulliver of his duty to return home. Gulliver thinks it better to return home and live as much of a recluse as he desires to be as he can not get an uninhabited island.

Gulliver Returns to England

Finally Gulliver, sad and grief-sticken, returns to England, much against his will. Gulliver's family is overjoyed to see him alive as they had taken him for dead. On the other hand, Gulliver is not happy to meet them as he is madly in love with the Houyhnhnms. He thinks of his family as Yahoos and cannot afford to be near them.

The thought that he had copulation with a female Yahoo and she begot three more Yahoos onto this earth, fills him with disgust and abhorrence. Even after having spent five years with his family, the spell of the Houyhnhnms remains unbroken and his wife and children are still Yahoos for him.

To compensate the tragic absence of the Houyhnhnms in his life, Gulliver buys two young stallions and spends at least four hours a day in the stables conversing with them.

Word Meaning

Desperate	– निराश	Fortunately	– सौभाग्य से
Retreat	– पीछे हटना	Visible	– दृश्य
Detestation	– घृणा	Poor	– निरीह
Strange	– विचित्र	Gratis	– नि:शुल्क

जहाज का कप्तान, Don Pedro de Mendez (डॉन पेड्रो डि मेंडेज), एक सच्चरित्र एवं उत्तम प्रकृति का व्यक्ति है, जो गुलिवर से अच्छा व्यवहार करता है। वह गुलिवर के विषय में सब कुछ जानने का प्रयत्न करता है, परंतु गुलिवर याहू प्राणियों से नफरत करने लगा था अत: वह स्वयं से जुड़ी कोई जानकारी नहीं देता है। वह याहू प्राणियों के आसपास भी नहीं रहना चाहता है। अत: बहुत-सी यात्राओं के दौरान वह अधिकांश समय अपने कक्ष में ही स्वयं को सीमित रखना पसंद करता है। वह सागर में छलांग लगाकर भागने का भी विचार करता है, परंतु अपने प्रयास के दौरान वह पकड़ लिया जाता है। डॉन पेड्रो को गुलिवर की कहानी पर सहसा विश्वास ही नहीं होता है, परंतु गुलिवर ने एक अरसे से न झूठ बोला है और न ही सुना है। गुलिवर कप्तान से वादा करता है कि वह लौटने के दौरान कोई आत्मघाती कदम नहीं उठाएगा। लिस्बन पहुँचकर डॉन पेड्रो गुलिवर को साथ रखने की इच्छा व्यक्त करता है। दस दिनों के पश्चात् डॉन पेड्रो गुलिवर को याद दिलाता कि उसे घर जाना चाहिए। गुलिवर सोचता है कि घर लौटकर अलग-अलग होकर जीवन-यापन करना उचित रहेगा और उसकी इच्छा भी है कि वह एकांत में रहे, परंतु उसे कोई निर्जन द्वीप नजर नहीं आता है।

गुलिवर का इंग्लैंड वापस लौट जाना

अंतत: गुलिवर दु:खी मन से इंग्लैंड लौट जाता है जिसके वह पूर्णत: अनिच्छुक था। गुलिवर का परिवार उसे सही सलामत लौटा हुआ देखकर अत्यंत प्रसन्न होता है, परंतु गुलिवर को अधिक प्रसन्नता नहीं होती, क्योंकि वह हायोम्स से बिछड़ना नहीं चाहता था। वह अपने परिवारजनों को याहू प्राणी समझता है एवं उनके साथ रहने से कतराने लगता है।

यह विचार कि उसने एक मादा याहू के साथ संबंध बनाकर तीन और याहू प्राणियों को जन्म दिया है, उसे घृणा एवं तिरस्कार की भावना से भर देता है। अपनी पत्नी एवं बच्चों के साथ पाँच वर्ष गुजारने के बावजूद वह सब उसके लिए याहू ही है तथा उसे स्वयं हायोम्स की याद सताती रहती है।

हायोम्स की कमी को पूरा करने हेतु गुलिवर दो नर घोड़े खरीद लेता है तथा प्रतिदिन वह चार घंटे उनसे संवाद करने में गुजारता है।

Sullen – क्रोधित
Offence – अपराध
Conceal – छिपाना
Defile – दूषित करना
Conspiracy – योजना (विशेषत: षड्यंत्र)
Inviolable – अलंघनीय
Observation – परीक्षण
Seduced – प्रेरित किया

Important Questions

Questions based on the Plot of the Chapter

Q 1. Describe Gulliver's dangerous voyage before he saw the Portuguese ship.

पुर्तगाली जहाज देखने से पूर्व गुलिवर की खतरों भरी समुद्र यात्रा का वर्णन कीजिए।

↗ गुलिवर का घोड़ों के द्वीप को छोड़कर जाने हेतु अनिच्छुक होना – घोड़ों के स्वामी की आज्ञा मानकर उसका दु:खी मन से द्वीप छोड़ना – उसके द्वारा एक निर्जन द्वीप की तलाश करना – उसे एक छोटा द्वीप नजर आना एवं वहाँ पर उसका डेरा डाल देना – उस द्वीप पर कई समस्याएँ होना – अपने ठहराव के चौथे दिन गुलिवर को कुछ द्वीपवासियों का नजर आना – द्वीपवासियों का विचित्र एवं नग्न अवस्था में होना।

Ans. Gulliver did not want to leave the island of horses, but because of the order of the master horse, he had to leave the island. After the instruction of the master horse, Gulliver left the island and set out towards a new destination. However, his journey was not easy because he was in search of an independent and uninhafited island to which he could not find out. After a long search, Gulliver found a small island and he decided to stay there for some days because of his extreme tiredness. He felt a lot of problems there because there was nothing to eat and he had to take limpets as food in order to keep himself alive. During the fourth day of stay, Gulliver saw some natives of that small island who were totally uncivilised and naked. Gulliver tried to escape from there, but a native attacked him with a poisoned arrow which was a horrible experience for Gulliver.

Q 2. Describe Gulliver's encounter with the Portuguese sailors.

पुर्तगाली नाविकों से गुलिवर का सामना किस प्रकार हुआ? वर्णन कीजिए।

↗ गुलिवर का नए ठिकाने की तलाश में होना तथा इसके लिए उसका किसी निर्जन द्वीप की तलाश करना – उसके द्वारा एक छोटे से द्वीप पर रुकने का निर्णय लिया जाना – उस द्वीप का अत्यंत विचित्र होना – एक द्वीपवासी द्वारा गुलिवर पर हमला किया जाना – उसे एक पुर्तगाली जहाज का नजर आना – गुलिवर का बच निकलने का प्रयत्न करना, परंतु अन्य नाविकों द्वारा उसे पकड़ लिया जाना – जहाज के कप्तान का एक अच्छा व्यक्ति होना – गुलिवर के विषय में जानने का यत्न करना गुलिवर के द्वारा कुछ भी न बताया जाना – गुलिवर का लंबी यात्रा के पश्चात् वापस इंग्लैंड जाना।

Ans. Gulliver wanted to stay somewhere and for this purpose, he searched any uninhabited island. However, he could not get an uninlabited island and he had to stay on a small island where he did not find any favourable condition. In addition to this, a native of that island attacked him also, so he tried to escape from there. He was in search of another destination, then he saw a Portuguese ship. He did not want to share the ship with Yahoos, so he wanted to go on other side of the island, but the sailors of that ship tracked him and presented him in front of their captain. The caption of that ship was a nice gentleman and he behaved in a well manner with Gulliver. The captain of that ship tried to know every detail about Gulliver, but because of his hate towards Yahoos, Gulliver did not share anything with him. Gulliver tried to escape from that ship also, but the sailors tracked him and he could not become successful in his attempts. Anyway, after a long journey, finally Gulliver returned to England.

Q 3. What was Gulliver's reaction when he met and lived with his family?

जब गुलिवर अपने परिवार से मिला तथा उनके साथ रहने लगा तो उसकी प्रतिक्रिया क्या रही?

गुलिवर का इंग्लैंड लौटने के प्रति अनिच्छुक होना – उसका वापस घोड़ों के द्वीप पर जाने को इच्छुक होना – उसका वापस घर लौटना एवं किसी प्रकार का उत्साह अनुभव ना करना – उसके परिवारजनों का अत्यंत प्रसंन होना – उसे निरंतर हायोम्स की याद आना – उसके द्वारा परिवार हेतु किसी भी प्रकार का आकर्षण अनुभव न किया जाना – इस कारण उसका अकेला एवं उदास होना – उसके द्वारा दो घोड़े लाए जाना।

Ans. Gulliver did not want to return England, but finally he had to do so because he was unable to wander here and there without any purpose. He wanted to go back to the island of the horses, but it was not proper to go there because of disapproval of other horses. However, when he returned to his family, he did not feel any special happiness whereas his family members became too happy when they saw him safe and alive. Gulliver found himself unable to connect with his family and with rest of things because he was feeling a strong bond of love with the horses. He began to hate Yahoos after meeting with the horses and he thought of his family as Yahoos that's why he could not afford to be near them. Except this, he started to curse himself because of giving birth to three more Yahoos.

The Tale of Adventures

Gulliver concludes the story of his adventures in Lilliput, Brobdingnag, Laputa and the land of the Houyhnhnms. Unlike those travellers who tamper their write-ups and distort the truth of their adventures, Gulliver's tale is complete true. His main motive behind writing his adventures is not to become famous, but make the world know of the great Houyhnhnms, free from all devices and cherubim of decency.

No Country is Worth to be Invaded

Gulliver is supposed to provide his narrative first of all to an English secretary of state so that to provide the Crown with an opportunity to attack the countries, the writer has been to and makes them a part of the British colonies. According to Gulliver, no country or island is worth to be attacked as Lilliputians are too small, the Brobdingnagians too large and dangerous, the Laputians, beyond the reach due to the floating island and Houyhnhnms unaware of the concept of war. Besides, they are agile and intelligent, who would quickly save their island by trampling the British. Instead, Gulliver wants the Houyhnhnms come over and teach the Europeans Yahoos all of their virtues.

Visualisation

Gulliver while sitting in the garden, visualises about the Houyhnhnms. He dreams of teaching his family the lessons he learnt on the island of the Houyhnhnms, looking at the mirror to be habitual to the features of Yahoos; lamenting the cruel disposition of the Houyhnhnms in England. When he returned from the land of the Houyhnhnms, he felt disgusted to have dinner at the same table with his family, but now it is not so as they have their meals together at the same table, although he is still teaching them to get rid of their vices.

12

साहसिक कारनामों के किस्से

गुलिवर Lilliput (लिलिपुट), Brobdingnag (ब्रॉबडिंगनाग), लापुता तथा हायोम्स की दुनिया के अपने साहसिक कारनामों के किस्से को समाप्त करता है। अन्य यात्रियों की भाँति गुलिवर किसी भी बात का बढ़ा-चढ़ाकर वर्णन न करते हुए अपनी सच्ची कहानियाँ ही दुनिया को बताने का निर्णय लेता है। गुलिवर का अपनी यात्राओं के विषय में लिखने का उद्देश्य विख्यात होना नहीं अपितु दुनिया को हायोम्स के विषय में बताना है, जो समाज की सभी प्रकार की बुराइयों से अलग हैं।

किसी भी राज्य का आक्रमण किए जाने योग्य न होना

गुलिवर को England (इंग्लैंड) के राजतंत्र की ओर से उसकी यात्राओं का पूर्ण विवरण देने का आदेश मिलता है। गुलिवर इंग्लैंड को अपनी सारी यात्राओं का विवरण देना चाहता है यद्यपि जब उसे राजतंत्र की मंशा का पता लगता है तो उसे थोड़ा अफसोस होता है क्योंकि राजतंत्र उन राज्यों पर आक्रमण करके उन्हें अपनी हुकूमत में शामिल करने हेतु आतुर था। गुलिवर के अनुसार किसी भी देश या द्वीप पर हमला करना व्यर्थ है क्योंकि लिलिपुट राज्य के निवासी अत्यंत छोटे हैं, ब्रॉबडिंगनाग राज्य के निवासी विशाल एवं खतरनाक हैं, लापुता राज्य के निवासी पहुँच के बाहर हैं तथा हायोम्स युद्ध की अवधारणा से पूरी तरह अनजान हैं। इसके अतिरिक्त वे सभी अत्यंत फुर्त एवं चतुर हैं जो British (ब्रिटिश) हुकूमत से अपने राज्यों की रक्षा करने में पूरी तरह सक्षम हैं। गुलिवर की इच्छा है कि हायोम्स आकर Europ (यूरोप) के याहू प्राणियों में सद्भाव एवं गुणों का प्रत्यारोपण करें।

मानसिक दर्शन

गुलिवर बगीचे में बैठकर Houyhnhnms (हायोम्स) के विषय में सोचने लगता है। वह सोचने लगता है कि उसे अपने परिवार को वे सारी शिक्षाएँ देनी चाहिए जो उसने हायोम्स के साथ रहते हुए प्राप्त की थीं, वह दर्पण में हायोम्स का प्रतिबिंब देखता है तथा मन-ही-मन में स्वयं को हायोम्स से जुड़ा हुआ पाता है, उसे इंग्लैंड में घोड़ों की दयनीय दशा पर अफसोस होता है। जब गुलिवर हायोम्स की दुनिया से वापस आया तो उसे अपने परिवार के साथ खाने की मेज पर बैठकर खाना खाने में आनंद नहीं आता था, परंतु अब ऐसा नहीं है क्योंकि अब वे एक साथ बैठकर उसी मेज पर खाना खाते हैं यद्यपि वह अब भी अपने परिवारजनों को नैतिकता की सीख दिया करता है।

Word Meaning

Tales	– किस्से	Improve	– सुधार
Voyages	– समुद्री यात्राएँ	Fabulous	– आश्चर्यजनक
Vogue	– चलन	Modesty	– विनम्रता
Justice	– न्याय	Missive	– विशालकाय
Fidelity	– भरोसा	Docible	– आज्ञाकारी
Tolerate	– सहन करना	Tincture	– रंग
Oblivion	– गुमनामी	Patience	– धैर्य
Experience	– अनुभव		

Important Questions

Questions based on the Plot of the Chapter

Q 1. What was the main motive behind Gulliver's writing?

गुलिवर का अपनी यात्रा वृत्तंत के वर्णन का मुख्य उद्देश्य क्या था?

↗ गुलिवर का अपने परिवार के पास लौटना परंतु संतुष्ट न होना – उसे घोड़ों की दुनिया की याद सताना – गुलिवर को याहू प्राणियों के दुर्गुणों पर क्रोध आना – गुलिवर द्वारा घोड़ों के गुणों का प्रचार किया जाना – गुलिवर का अपनी समुद्री यात्रा का विवरण करना – गुलिवर का याहू प्राणियों को नैतिकता एवं मानवता का पाठ पढ़ाने का इच्छुक होना – गुलिवर का स्वयं की ख्याति हेतु उत्सुक न होना – गुलिवर का अपने अनुभवों का एवं घोड़ों के सद्गुणों का सत्यतापूर्ण लेखन करना।

Ans. Gulliver returned to his family, but he was not feeling satisfied because he wanted to live with those virtuous horses. Gulliver did not like the world of Yahoos because the Yahoos were full of various types of vices and they were very proudy. Gulliver wanted to advertise the virtues of the horses and he decided to do so by writing his experience of encounter with those virtuous horses. Gulliver was very depressed because of the situation of Yahoos in the English society as all of them were involved in cheating one another and collecting more and more luxuries for themselves. Gulliver wanted to teach them the lesson of morality and inner satisfaction, so he decided to present all the virtues of horses in form of writing of his voyage. Gulliver was not concerned for own name and fame because he was not a greedy person. Gulliver explained all his experiences with full accuracy and truthfulness so that it could be exemplary for every Yahoo.

Q 2. Why Gulliver was not in favour of war with any state where he had visited?

गुलिवर ने जिन राज्यों की यात्रा की वह उनमें से किसी भी राज्य से युद्ध के पक्ष में क्यों नहीं था?

गुलिवर का उत्तम प्रकृति का व्यक्ति होना तथा घोड़ों के द्वीप की यात्रा के पश्चात् उसका शांतिवादी हो जाना – गुलिवर का घोड़ों के सद्गुणों को अपनाने हेतु इच्छुक होना – गुलिवर का इंग्लैंड के अधिकारियों को अपनी यात्राओं के विषय में बताना – गुलिवर का अधिकारियों को युद्ध न करने हेतु मनाने का प्रयास करना – गुलिवर का बताना कि किसी भी राज्य पर हमला करना व्यर्थ है – गुलिवर का बताना कि सभी प्राणियों का चालाक, फुर्त एवं अपने राज्यों की रक्षा करने में पूर्णतः समर्पित होना – गुलिवर का युद्ध विरोधी होना।

Ans. Gulliver was a nice person and he became completely pacifist after his visit to the island of horses. Gulliver wanted to adopt all the virtues of horses and for this, he was ready to change himself completely. When he reported his journey details to the empire of England, the English administration began to plan for invading all the states where Gulliver had travelled.

However, when Gulliver observed this scheme of English officials, he became very sad, but he decided to convince them for no war. He told the officials that no country was worth to be attacked because the Lilliputians were too small, the Brobdingnagians were too large and dangerous, the Laputians were beyond to reach and the Houyhnhnms were not aware of the concept of war.

Gulliver further added that all those creatures were too agile and intelligent to be defeated or enslaved. Gulliver was not in favour of any type of violence or disturbance, so he did so. Expectations of Gulliver were quite true and genuine because war is good for nothing.

QUESTIONS DIGEST

Term II

Questions based on the Plot

Q 1. Describe Gulliver's meeting with the two horses. How were the dapple grey and the other horse different from the ordinary horses?

गुलिवर की घोड़ों से हुई मुलाकात का वर्णन करिए? किस प्रकार से वे दो घोड़े अन्य घोड़ों से भिन्न थे?

Ans. When the ugly animals were pestering Gulliver, all of a sudden they ran away. The cause of their sudden disappearance was a horse. Gulliver saw a dapple grey horse walking gently in the field. The horse stared at Gulliver with wonder. When Gulliver tried to stroke the horse, he did not receive it like the other horses, he rather disliked the civilities offered by Gulliver. The way he neighed had a particular cadence in it and sounded like a language.

At that time, another horse came up and the two horses behaved, so rationally with each other that Gulliver felt that the inhabitants of that country must be the wisest people on Earth. The two horses observed Gulliver minutely conveying all traces of reason. It made Gulliver wonder that they were some magicians, who had transformed themselves on some purpose. They frequently repeated the word 'Yahoo.' Gulliver, at last, thought it prudent to follow the directions of the dapple grey horse.

Q 2. How did Gulliver manage to have a proper diet in the Houyhnhnm country? What did he feel about it?

हायोम्स के राष्ट्र में (राज्य में) गुलिवर ने किस प्रकार अपने लिए उचित भोजन का प्रबन्ध किया? उसे ये भोजन कैसा लगा तथा उस पर इसका क्या प्रभाव रहा?

Ans. At first, Gulliver was at a loss regarding his food. Then he thought of making a kind of bread out of oats. He had initially declined the oats as it was not his food. He heated, grounded and beat oats to make a paste and to as ted the paste at the fire and ate it warm with milk. Initially, Gulliver found it tasteless but got used to it with time. Gulliver supplemented his staple diet occasionally with a rabbit or bird, herbs, butter and whey. In the beginning, Gulliver felt a strong need of salt, but soon came to enjoy his food without salt. He came to think of salt as a luxury introduced as a provocative to drink. Gulliver felt the good effects of this diet on his health, he had never had any sickness in the entire course of his stay in the island.

Q 3. Give an account of the way in which Gulliver learned the language of the Houyhnhnms.

गुलिवर ने किस प्रकार हायोम्स की भाषा सीखी, संक्षेप में वर्णन करिए?

Ans. Gulliver's main aim was to learn the language of the Houyhnhnms. Everyone in the household of the master horse was eager to teach him because they considered it a great achievement in a brute animal to possess signs of rationality. Gulliver pointed to different things to inquire their names and made notes of things he learned. He repeated those names with the help of the family members to improve his accent. The master horse was very curious to know about Gulliver and devoted many hours to instruct him. Gulliver, on his part, made a good effort to learn the language, he formed everything he learned into the English alphabet, wrote the words and their translations. All this had the effect of making Gulliver reasonably well in understanding and expressing himself in their language in a short span of five months.

Q 4. Describe the assessment given by Gulliver to the master horse about the institution of law and lawyers.

न्याय एवं अधिवक्ताओं के संस्थान का मूल्यांकन गुलिवर ने किस प्रकार घोड़ों के स्वामी के समक्ष प्रस्तुत किया?

Ans. Gulliver told his master that law was a science, which was practised by a society of men called lawyers. Their training consisted in twisting and fabricating the truth and facts. They dwelt on useless matters related to circumstances rather than merits of the case and took a very long time in deciding a case. They had a special interest in keeping records and on the basis of such records passed precedents to justify the most unjust opinions.

The language used by them was so complex that only they could understand it and they adapted this language to their own advantage in such a way that it totally confused the notions of truth and falsehood, right and wrong. Only in the cases involving crimes against the state, the method used was short and praiseworthy.

Q 5. Despite having a very aute judgement, the master horse listened to Gulliver's accounts with uneasiness. Explain.

तीव्र निर्णय क्षमता होने के बावजूद घोड़ों के स्वामी ने गुलिवर की बातों को चिन्ता पूर्वक क्यों सुना? विस्तार पूर्वक समझाइए?

Ans. The master horse listened to Gulliver with uneasiness as his conceptions were totally logical, straightforward and upright. During his conversation with Gulliver, he could not comprehend it when Gulliver referred to the nature of manhood and its faculty of lying and falsehood. Lying and falsehood were totally strange notions to his virtuous nature. For him, speech served the basic purpose of understanding one another and receiving information of facts. But if someone said thing that was not, the entire purpose was defeated. His notions were devoid of any idea that the speech could be manipulated.

Q 6. State the impressions formed by the master horse about human beings after listening to Gulliver's account.

गुलिवर की बातें सुनने के पश्चात् घोड़ों के स्वामी ने मानवों के प्रति किस प्रकार की प्रतिक्रिया प्रदर्शित की?

Ans. After analysing the account given by Gulliver about his country and countrymen, the masterhorse drew some serious observations on the human beings. He thought of human beings as some sort of animals, who were provided with a little reason by nature. But the human beings chose to use this faculty of reason to increase their natural vices and to acquire the new ones that nature had not given them, but which were the product of their own making.

The human beings further denied themselves of the few abilities given by nature and excelled in increasing their wants. As a result, their entire life was spent in useless efforts to satisfy those unnecessary wants.

Q 7. Give an account of the general life of the Houyhnhnms: their nature institution of marriage, manner of educating their young ones.

हायोम्स के सामान्य जीवन का वर्णन करिए? उनकी प्रकृति, वैवाहिक संस्था, शिक्षा विधि इत्यादि बिंदुओं पर प्रकाश डालिए।

Ans. The Houyhnhnms were virtuous, rational and just. Their rationality was not tampered with any emotion or passion. Their principal virtues of friendship and benevolence had universal application for them. They observed decency and civility, but had no place for formality. They had no particular attachments to their own families and children but had general affection towards the whole species. Their marriages took place on the basis of preserving their race and the married couples lived peacefully throughout their lives. They had no place for emotions and passions. Their method of educating their young ones was admirable. Their children led a very simple and disciplined life and observed temperance, industry, exercise and cleanliness. They trained their young ones to acquire strength and speed and regular meets were held for youth to show their skills. Every fourth year, they held a representative council of the nation to inquire into the state and condition of districts. In such meetings, deficient state was supplied with anything it lacked and also the regulation of children was settled in order to maintain an equilibrium in the society.

Q 8. The master horse had to send Gulliver away from the Houyhnhnm country. What were the circumstances that compelled the master to do this and how did it affect Gulliver?

घोड़ों के स्वामी को गुलिवर को हायोम्स समाज से दूर भेजना पड़ा। किस परिस्थितियों में घोड़ों का स्वामी ऐसा करने को विवश हुआ एवं इसका गुलिवर पर क्या प्रभाव पड़ा?

Ans. At the General Assembly, the representatives took an offence that the master horse was keeping and treating a Yahoo, that is, Gulliver, like a Houyhnhnm than as a brute animal. It was considered unseasonable and unnatural. The assembly decided that either the Gulliver would be made to work like the other Yahoos or would be sent away from the island. Due to the pressure on the master, he had no choice but to carry out the order of the assembly. Gulliver was completely shattered at this and fainted due to the shock he received. He was utterly griefed and contemplated death better than the fate he had been assigned to. The very idea of spending his life with the Yahoos appeared to him as the worst thing.

Q 9. How did the Houyhnhnms treat death? What does it show about them?

हायोम्स मृत्यु की किस प्रकार विवेचना करते थे? यह उनके विषय में क्या दर्शाता है?

Ans. The Houyhnhnms treated death just as a common natural occurance. They did not express any emotion on the death of their friends and relatives. They generally lived till the age of seventy or seventy five years. Even the dying person did not bother about leaving the world. The dying person merely felt a decay some weeks before death and was visited by his friends. He even made the returns visits to his neighbours about ten days before death. They remained calm and composed at the approach of death. It is evident by their attitude towards the death that they had attained a very high degree of rationality and accepted the laws of nature with utmost dignity and composure.

Questions Based on the Character Sketch

Q 10. Gulliver makes a scathing criticism of his society is the descriptions of his country to the master horse. What traits of Gulliver's characters are revealed by this?

गुलिवर अपने समाज की आलोचना करता है तथा अपने समाज का विकृत रूप घोड़ों के स्वामी के सम्मुख रखता है। इससे उसका कौन-सा गुण परिलक्षित होता है?

Ans. The account given by Gulliver shows that he had a great capacity of mind and deep understanding of human nature and its vices. He was fully aware of the evils affecting his society, the vanities of the upper class and the desperation of the deprived class for existence. He was against the system that made a few enjoy the riches and luxury and deprived the rest large number of people even of the basic necessities of life. He attacked the corruption prevalent in every institution of the society, when he laid bare the practices of different classes: of government, professionals and aristocracy. He acted like a reformist and held a mirror up to the society of his times. It is evident from his description that was a just, balanced and wise human being driven by the humane considerations of justice and morality.

Q 11. Give your opinions about Gulliver's master, the Great Houyhnhnm.

गुलिवर के स्वामी महान् हायोम के विषय में अपने विचार व्यक्त करिए?

Ans. In the introduction of the master horse itself, as the dapple grey horse, the impression that comes to mind is of a distinguished and regal horse. He was rational, logical with a very acute judgement. He was an epitome of virtues and was at a loss in understanding human faculties of lying, falsehood etc due to his very well developed sense of rationality and strait forward, clear notions. He was also of curious nature and wanted to know about Gulliver. So, he instructed him in his language. He did not react to Gulliver's accounts in haste, but logically arrived at his conclusions. His hospitality is evident from the kindness with which he treated Gulliver. He was indeed very intelligent with deep understanding.

Q 12. On returning home, Gulliver came to enjoy the company of the two horses much more than he had ever enjoyed the human company. What changes did he undergo in his personality? Explain.

घर लौटने पर गुलिवर को दो घोड़ों का साथ अत्यंत पसंद आया जबकि उसे मानवों का साथ भी इतना पसंद नहीं आया था। उसके व्यक्तित्व में किस प्रकार के परिवर्तन हुए थे?

Ans. After living for three years in the country of the Houyhnhnms, Gulliver was a completely changed man. He endeavoured to cultivate in himself the virtues he learnt under the influence of the Houyhnhnms. During the first year after his coming back home, he resented even the company of his family. He first of all bought two stone-hores and he felt a strong bond of friendship with them. These changes were the result of his longing for the Houyhnhnms and the sense of loss he felt due to his separation from them. He did not want to return to the ways of life of the Yahoos or the humans. The horses reaffirmed his faith in the virtues and the high conduct of the Houyhnhnms. Gulliver desired nothing more than upholding those virtues and ideals.

Character Sketches

Gulliver

The narrator and protagonist of the story. Although Lemuel Gulliver's vivid and detailed style of narration makes it clear that he is intelligent and well - educated, his perceptions are naïve and gullible. He has virtually no emotional life, or at least no awareness of it and his comments are strictly factual. Indeed, sometimes his obsession with the facts of navigation, for example, becomes unbearable for us, as his fictional editor, Richard Sympson, makes clear when he explains having had to cut out nearly half of Gullivers verbiage. Gulliver never thinks that the absurdities he encounters are funny and never makes the satiric connections between the lands he visits and his own home. Gullivers naïveté makes the satire possible, as we pick up on things that Gulliver does not notice.

The Emperor

The ruler of Lilliput. Like all Lilliputians, the emperor is fewer than six inches tall. His power and majesty impress Gulliver deeply, but to us he appears both laughable and sinister. Because of his tiny size, his belief that he can control Gulliver seems silly, but his willingness to execute his subjects for minor reasons of politics or honour gives him a frightening aspect. He is proud of possessing the tallest trees and biggest palace in the kingdom, but he is also quite hospitable, spending a fortune on his captives food. The emperor is both a satire of the autocratic ruler and a strangely serious portrait of political power.

The Farmer

Gullivers first master in Brobdingnag. The farmer speaks to Gulliver, showing that he is willing to believe that the relatively tiny Gulliver may be as rational as he himself is, and treats him with gentleness. However, the farmer puts Gulliver on display around Brobdingnag, which clearly shows that he would rather profit from his discovery than converse with him as an equal. His exploitation of Gulliver as a labourer, which nearly starves Gulliver to death, seems less cruel than simple minded.

चरित्र चित्रण

गुलिवर

कथावाचक एवं कहानी का मुख्य नायक। यद्यपि लैमुअल गुलिवर के कथा कहने के तरीके से पता चलता है कि वह भली-भाँती शिक्षित एवं दूरदर्शी सोच वाला व्यक्ति है किन्तु कहीं-कहीं उसके विचार उसके अनुभवहीन एवं सरल व्यक्तित्व वाला होने की पुष्टि करते हैं। आभासी रुप से उसकी कोई भावनात्मक जिंदगी नहीं अथवा उसे भावनाओं का कोई ज्ञान नहीं है एवं उसके विचार पूर्ण रुप से तार्किक हैं। वास्त में कहीं-कहीं नौका विज्ञान से उसके लगाव से संबंधित तथ्य हमें बोझिल लगने लगते हैं परन्तु उसके संपादक रिचर्ड सिंपसन का प्रस्तुतीकरण विषय को सहज बनाता है जिसमें उस संपादक ने गुलिवर के अनावश्यक विचारों को पृथक कर दिया है। गुलिवर कभी यह नहीं सोचता कि वह जिन विषमताओं का सामना कर रहा है, वे हास्यास्पद हैं तथा वह कभी भी उन परिस्थितियों की अपने गृहनगर से व्यंग्यपूर्ण तुलना भी नहीं करता है। यद्यपि गुलिवर की सरलता व्यंग्य का अवसर उत्पन्न करती है, विशेष रुप से उन बातों के संदर्भ में जिन पर गुलिवर का ध्यान नहीं जाता।

बादशाह

लिलिपुर का बादशाह, एवं अन्य लिलिपुर वासियों की भाँति बादशाह भी छः इंच से कम लम्बाई वाला है। उसकी ताकत एवं सत्ता गुलिवर को प्रभावित करती है परन्तु हमारे लिये वह हँसी का पात्र तथा डरावना पात्र है। उसके छोटे कद के बावजूद उसका विश्वास, कि वह गुलिवर को नियंत्रित कर लेगा, मूर्खतापूर्ण लगता है परन्तु राजनीति या सम्मान से जुड़े छोटे मुद्दों पर भी अपराधियों का मृत्युदंड देने की उसकी प्रवृत्ति उसे डरावना बनाती है। उसे अपने साम्राज्य में सबसे बड़े होने पर गर्व है तथा उसका राज्य बड़ा है, इस बात का भी उसे गर्व है परन्तु वह अपने बंदी बनाये हुए व्यक्तियों के भोजन पर उदारतापूर्वक व्यय करता है जो उसकी उदार मनोवृत्ति का परिचायक है। बादशाह एक तानाशाही शासक तथा राजनैतिक शक्ति का प्रतीक दोनों ही है।

कृषक

ब्राब्डिगनैग में गुलिवर का प्रथम स्वामी। कृषक गुलिवर से बातें करता है तथा यह प्रदर्शित करता है कि वह यह स्वीकार करने को राजी है कि कद में अत्यंत छोटा गुलिवर भी उसकी तरह ही आनुपातिक व्यवहार वाला हो सकता है तथा कृषक उसके प्रति यशोचित व्यवहार करता है। यद्यपि बाद में कृषक गुलिवर को प्रदर्शनी हेतु रखता है जिससे यह स्पष्ट हो जाता है कि ह गुलिर से समतापूर्ण व्यवहार करने के स्थान पर उससे लाभ कमाना अधिक पसंद करेगा। उसका गुलिवर के प्रति शोषणकारी व्यवहार जो कि लगभग गुलिवर को मृत्यु तक ले जाता है, हमें

Generally, the farmer represents the average Brobdingnagian of no great gifts or intelligence, wielding an extraordinary power over Gulliver simply by virtue of his immense size.

Glumdalclitch

The farmers nine years old daughter, who is forty feet tall. Glumdalclitch becomes Gullivers friend and nurse-maid, hanging him to sleep safely in her closet at night and teaching him the Brobdingnagian language by day. She is skilled at sewing and makes Gulliver several sets of new clothes, taking delight in dressing him. When the queen discovers that no one at court is suited to care for Gulliver, she invites Glumdalclitch to live at court as his sole babysitter, a function she performs with great seriousness and attentiveness. To Glumdalclitch, Gulliver is basically a living doll, symbolising the general status Gulliver has in Brobdingnag.

The Queen

The queen of Brobdingnag, who is so delighted by Gulliver's beauty and charms that she agrees to buy him from the farmer for 1000 pieces of gold. Gulliver appreciates her kindness after the hardships he suffers at the farmer's and shows his usual fawning love for royalty by kissing the tip of her little finger when presented before her. She possesses, in Gullivers words, "infinite" wit and humour, though this description may entail a bit of Gullivers characteristic flattery of superiors. The queen seems genuinely considerate, asking Gulliver whether he would consent to live at court instead of simply taking him in as a pet and inquiring into the reasons for his cold good-byes with the farmer. She is by no means a hero, but simply a pleasant, powerful person.

सामान्य रुप से सोचने पर अधिक क्रूरतापूर्ण नहीं प्रतीत होता है। सामान्य रुप से कहा जाये तो गुलिवर का स्वामी कृषक एक सामान्य ब्राब्डिगनैग वासी है जिसके पास कोई अतिरिक्त विशेषता नहीं है तथा उसे अपने असाधारण आकार के कारण ही गुलिवर से अधिक शक्ति प्राप्त है।

ग्लमडैलक्लिच

कृषक की नौ वर्षीय पुत्री जिसका कद 40 फीट है। ग्लमडैलक्लिच गुलिवर की मित्र एवं सहायक परिचारिका बन जाती है तथा वह उसे उसकी सुरक्षा हेतु रात में अपने पलंग में सुलाती है तथा दिन में उसे ब्रॉब्डिगनैग की भाषा सिखाती है। उसे सिलाई कला में दक्षता प्राप्त है तथा वह गुलिवर के लिये कई नये कपड़े सिलती है तथा इस कार्य में उसे आनन्द प्राप्त होता है। जब रानी को यह ज्ञात हो जाता है कि दरबार में कोई भी गुलिवर का ध्यान ठीक तरह से रख सकने में सक्षम नहीं है तो वह ग्लमडैलक्लिच को दरबार में आने का निमंत्रण देती है तथा उसे गुलिवर की देख-रेख की जिम्मेदारी सौंपती है जिसे ग्लमडैलक्लिच पूरी तन्मयता तथा गंभीरता के साथ निभाती है। ग्लमडैलक्लिच हेतु गुलिवर एक जीती-जागती गुड़िया है तथा ब्रॉब्डिगनैग में गुलिवर की सामान्य पहचान भी यही है।

रानी

ब्रॉब्डिगनैग की रानी गुलिवर की सुंदरता एवं उसके आकर्षण से अत्यधिक सम्मोहित हो जाती है तथा वह उसे 1,000 स्वर्ण मुद्राओं के बदले कृषक से खरीद लेती है। गुलिवर रानी की दयालुता की प्रशंसा करता है तथा कृषक के द्वारा किये गये क्रूर व्यवहार के पश्चात् जब उसे रानी का स्नेहपूर्ण व्यवहार मिलता है तो वह भावविहवल हो जाता है। जब उसे रानी के समक्ष प्रस्तुत किया जाता है तब वह रानी की छोटी उंगली का चुंबन लेकर रानी के प्रति अपने प्रेम व आदर को प्रकट करता है। गुलिवर के शब्दों में रानी के पास ''असाधारण बृद्धि एवं विनोदप्रियता'' थी, यद्यपि यह विवरण हमें गुलिवर के विशिष्ट व्यक्तियों की चापलूसी करने के स्वाभाव की थोड़ी सी झलक भी देता है। रानी पर्याप्त रुप से विचारशील है क्योंकि वह गुलिवर से पूछती है कि क्या वह दरबार में रहना पसंद करेगा बजाय इसके कि वह पालतु बन कर रानी के साथ रहे तथा वह उससे उसके कृषक के प्रति रुखे व्यवहार के विषय में भी पूछती है। वह किसी भी प्रकार से नायिका नहीं है परन्तु वह एक आनन्ददायक तथा शक्तिशाली व्यक्तित्व की स्वामिनी है।

www.ingramcontent.com/pod-product-compliance
Ingram Content Group UK Ltd.
Pitfield, Milton Keynes, MK11 3LW, UK
UKHW021659190726
13853UKWH00001B/368